BACK TALK
for GRANDPARENTS
(and their grandchildren)

20 ways to stop rude behavior
before it hurts their relationship

Audrey Ricker, Ph.D

AMAGANSETT
PUBLISHING

Published by Amagansett Publishing, LLC, Waxhaw, NC. Amagansett Publishing is a registered trademark of Amagansett Publishing, LLC. The Amagansett Publishing boat logo is a trademark of Amagansett Publishing, LLC.

Printed in the United States of America

Cover design by Ellie Leacock, Arttstuff Design

Publisher's Cataloging-in-Publication
(Provided by Quality Books, Inc.)

Ricker, Audrey.
    Backtalk for grandparents and their grandchildren: 20 ways to stop rude behavior before it hurts the relationship / Audrey Ricker. — 1st ed.
        p.   cm.
    Includes index.
    LCCN: 2001116680
    ISBN:0-9708875-0-7

    1. Grandparent and child. 2. Discipline of children. 3. Grandparenting. 4. Respect.   I. Title.

BF723.G68R53   2001   649'.64
QBI01-200412

This book is dedicated to

Audrey Marcus,
Grandmother *Extraordinaire*

for her knowledge, wisdom,
honesty and spiritual insight.

Table
of Contents

INTRODUCTION
Backtalk for Grandparents and
Their Grandchildren: *Twenty Ways
to Stop Rudeness From Ruining
Their Relationship* vii

ACKNOWLEDGEMENTS xi

PART I
Backtalk: *What it is, How
Grandparents Can Deal With It
The Four Steps Are Explained* 1

Chapter One
Why I Wrote This Book 3

Chapter Two
The Special Time 7

Chapter Three
Let the Bad Times Begin! 11

Chapter Four
The Four Steps Reviewed 15

Chapter Five
Step One: Recognize the Backtalk 21

Chapter Six
*Step Two: Choosing a
Consequence for the Backtalk* 29

Chapter Seven
*Step Three: Enacting
the Consequence* 39

Chapter Eight
*Step Four: Disengage
from the Protest* 43

PART II
*Sixteen Ways to Keep Rudeness
From Ruining the Grandparent-
Grandchild Relationship* 49

Chapter Nine
*Treat Your Grandchildren Better
Than You Did Your Children* 51

Chapter Ten
*Get a Life: Another Life
Besides the One You Devote
to Your Grandchildren* 55

Chapter Eleven
Set Your Own Rules 59

Chapter Twelve
Set Your Own Standards 61

Chapter Thirteen
Do Some Research 65

Chapter Fourteen
Don't Be a Sugar Pusher! 69

Chapter Fifteen
Model Peaceful Behavior 73

Chapter Fifteen
Set a Budget 77

Chapter Sixteen
Don't Play Favorites 83

Chapter Seventeen
Get Physical! 87

PART III

*How to Have a Rudeness-Free
Home That Your Grandchildren
Will Love Visiting* 89

Introduction 93

Chapter Eighteen
*Use Consistency in Your
Interactions With Grandchildren* 99

Chapter Nineteen
*Modeling Behavior You Expect
Your Grandchild to Display* 99

Chapter Twenty
Reinforcement 105

Chapter Twenty-One
Showing Empathy 111

Chapter Twenty-Two
  Caring for Plants,
  Animals and Things 117

Chapter Twenty-Three
  Show Genuine Love and Concern 119

Chapter Twenty Four
  Questions From, and Answers For,
  Grandparents About Dealing with
  Backtalk from Grandchildren 123

Chapter Twenty-Five
  Special Situations 131
  Handling backtalk when you're a
  step-grandparent. Dealing with backtalk
  when you're taking the grandchildren
  on a car trip. And much more...

Chapter Twenty-Six
  Workbook 139

Annotated List of Resources 145

Appendix
  Handling Backtalkers of All Ages
  from Toddlers to Age Twenty
  and Beyond. How to Start a
  Grandparent's Support Group.
  A Review of the Four Steps
  and the Calmes Plan 147

Index 161

Introduction

**Backtalk for Grandparents
and Their Grandchildren:
Twenty Ways to Stop Rudeness
from Ruining Their Relationship**

HELLO, GRANDPARENTS! I cannot say enough to praise you. You are known for road trips, woodworking lessons, trips to zoos, aquariums and antique doll stores. And talk – you are known for your conversations, your patient explanations, your willingness to listen to what kids have to say.

A sociologist concerned with the intrusion of technology into children's lives recently cried on a CNN news show, "Kids need humans!" You are the best kind of humans kids can get.

And you do not deserve some of the treatment from grandchildren that you are getting, or that you might get if you are not experiencing it already. And alas, you almost certainly will be treated rudely by at least some of your grandchildren because more kids are rude today. Some don't know they're being rude, some don't care if they're being rude, some think they should be rude.

Whatever the reason for it, the rudeness can hurt your happiness with those children, a lot.

How this book will help:

This book does, indeed, discuss twenty ways to keep rudeness from hurting the bond between grandchildren and grandparents.

The first four ways are the Four Steps (Part I) for ending backtalk that are mentioned in the book about backtalk I co-authored in 1998 (Simon and Schuster/Fireside).

The next ten ways (Part II) are based on my own research and stories I've gleaned from grandparents.

The last six ways (Part III) are the six strategies found in Educational Psychologist Robert E. Calmes' plan for communicating values to children, values that involve rudeness-free, loving, caring behavior. The Calmes' values education system is based on over 2000 research studies on childrearing. At the end of the 20 ways is a Question and Answer section based on specific questions from grandparents and a workbook chapter, to help you organize the material in this book so you can use it easily and keep track of how it worked. There are some e-mail addresses for me and Dr. Calmes. Also, there's a list of resources – other books – you might want to use.

The Appendix tells you how to deal with balktalkers from the age of toddlers on up, plus provides a review of the steps and suggestions for starting a grandparents' support group.

By using even some of the 20 ways listed here, grandparents can provide a happy, tension-free environment for children when they are not backtalking. In children's own homes, where parents fight exhaustion from working all the time and worrying about finances, children never know the kind of stress-free, peaceful environment that grand-parents can provide. It's not that the kids' homes are battlefields, exactly, but more like baseball dugouts in which everyone is resting up for his or her next try at school, sports, or work. Like the baseball players, the family's members work together but tend to live separate lives. It's not that grandparents don't have separate lives, but that they are at a stage to make the grand kids a priority.

According to the Amazon.com reviews of *Backtalk: Four Steps to Ending Rude Behavior in Kids,* the value of that book is in the explanations of the four steps. The value of this book is how you can use the four steps in your role as grandparents – that delicate role balanced between parent and friend.

Acknowledgments

I AM EXTREMELY GRATEFUL for the collaboration of Dr. Robert Calmes, and the delightful encouragement of Anne Campbell and Ellie Leacock.

And of course, I am ever indebted to the staff at Art Stuff for the brilliant cover those talented people designed and produced.

As always, my darling grandchildren continue to inspire me to be the best grandmother I can be.

I want to thank my neighbor, John Garland, for his constant encouragement and support.

And, of course, this book would not have been completed without Sally Rogers of Red Horse Graphics, Inc., and Elizabeth Felicetti of Felicetti Literary Services.

PART I:
BACKTALK

What it is, how grandparents can deal with it.

The Four Steps are explained.

Dear Grandma,

You have been the best to me since the day I was born. I have always enjoyed what we have done together. Do you remember the day I had a spraind foot and you took me to Paint Yourself Silly. I had so much fun. Thats the day you painted the fish and I painta multi color warm. Than there was the time you took Melissa and I to Hungry Hunter befor dance for my birthday gift.

Now you cant forget the time that you and me went to a gardening store and got a bunch of flowers and planted them in your backyard, and than you tought me how to hose the backyard down.

How wonderful can the grandparent-grandchild relationship be? Here is a terrific example of how wonderful, in a note (unsolicited!) sent to my friend, Audrey Marcus, by her granddaughter, Michelle, then aged ten.

Chapter One

Why I Wrote This Book

IN DOING INTERVIEWS and booksignings for my first book, *Backtalk: Four Steps to Ending Rude Behavior in Kids,* I heard from a lot of grandparents. "Our grandchildren are terrible!" they said. "Will your book help us stop backtalk from our grandchildren?"

I said it would.

But the truth is, I decided, grandparents need their own book. They're in a special category. The grandparent-grandchild relationship has its own set of rules.

Here are just a few:
1. Grandparents are meant to spoil kids rotten.
2. Grandparents are meant to have fun with their grandchildren.
3. Grandparents are meant to adore these special darlings unconditionally.
   In return, the grandchildren are supposed to love and adore their grandparents.

But today, kids often take the spoiling, the fun, and the unconditional love for granted. Instead of returning it in kind, they return it with backtalk – undeserved, rude, mean backtalk.

Why? There are lots of reasons, such as:

- Many kids honestly believe that backtalking is the way kids should communicate with adults.
- Other kids backtalk.
- Rudeness is a way of controlling all situations.
- Parents allow their children to get away with backtalking.
- Kids' TV shows, films, music, and especially their video games, feature backtalking nonstop. A new video game for girls features young ladies hurling insults at one another on school grounds. Players compete in teams to see who can hurl the most hurtful, harmful insults of all.
- It's a way for kids to feel they can assert themselves.

Grandparents I spoke with were hurt by this rude behavior from their darlings. As a result, they were trying to ignore it. They were also giving in to it, pleading with the children to stop it, and giving even more presents and treats in hopes of forestalling it – all of which are not only not going to work, but are likely to encourage more rude behavior from kids.

What grandparents have to do, I realized, is prepare themselves to handle backtalk not just when it happens but before it happens. That way they won't be taken so completely off guard. So, I decided to write a book for all grandparents, regardless of how polite their grandchildren seem.

But I don't want to start this book with backtalk bashing. First, I want to emphasize how wonderful the grandparent/grandchild relationship is!

Chapter Two

The Special Time

IN THE PROCESS of writing *Backtalk* and experiencing the unexpectedly huge, nationwide reception it got, I became something of a hardcase. "Yes, two-year-olds can backtalk!" I told eager listeners, talk show callers and lecture audiences. And then, giddy from the amazed reactions, I would elaborate. "You may think that the 'No' stage of a two year old is natural – but it's really backtalk, and you have to stop it then and there or your child will grow up to be a tyrant! Is that what you want? No!" Audiences – especially parents of kidlets just entering the Terrible Twos – seemed very happy to hear such pronouncements, so I pronounced them frequently, often with the zeal of a fire and brimstone preacher.

And, I would add frequently, "Don't let grandparents or other well-meaning but weak-willed relatives tell you any differently!" (My own mother had been a spoil-her-grandsons-rotten grandmother; I'd vowed I would never be like her with my grandchildren, ever.)

So, imagine *my* amazement to discover that my own two granddaughters – then aged one and three – were incapable of backtalking.

Nothing they *said* could be construed as rude! Assertive, yes! Strong, yes, even defiant – but never rude. Here they were, saying things that I had listed in my first book as backtalk. And look! From these darlings, such utterances were not backtalk at all!

For instance:

When my youngest grandchild, Gia, told me "No! Go 'way! Not my mommie!" (a specific example of backtalk according to what I wrote in the original *Backtalk* book) I gasped with delight at her confidence. "You surely can take care of yourself!" I told her approvingly, "never let anyone take that away from you, ever." Rude? No, she was being adorable – a tiny Gloria Bunker asserting herself with Archie.

And nothing these little granddaughters of mine *did* could be construed as bad behavior in any way.

For instance:

One day when I called my son and daughter-in-law's home, my oldest grand-daughter, Maria, was crying loudly because she had been forcibly stopped from pulling her sister's hair. "Oh, Grandma Audrey," Maria said sadly when she was put on the phone to talk to me, "I accidently pulled Gia's hair."

"Don't worry, darling," I heard myself say soothingly, "I sometimes accidentally pull people's hair, too."

"I like talking to you, Grandma Audrey," my precious said then, melting my heart in happiness thick as chocolate sauce.

And that's what being a grandmother is all about – total understanding of how wonderful, how perfect, how good, this child really is.

At the time I'm writing this book, my granddaughters are almost three and five. Their presence in the world has given me a joy I never knew I could feel. Time spent with them is magical. Every minute is a new experience in love and fun.

This is how it's supposed to be. As people say, it's much more fun being a grandparent than being a parent. And you just expect that fun to go on and on, for the rest of your life.

That was then, this is now.

Today, though, that expectation is not realistic. Thanks to the rude behavior allowed in our society, grandparents have to be prepared mentally and emotionally for the first backtalk attack from these children they love more than anyone in the world. If they're not, they'll be devastated for days, even weeks after the backtalk attack occurs; and so weakened emotionally they'll have no defenses for the second attack and all the others after that. This kind of weakness is not good for the parents, the grandparents – or, especially, for the grandchildren themselves!

Now, on with the one thing grandparents can do immediately to make sure that backtalk attack is handled as soon as it happens – and joy, not rudeness, runs this most special of all relationships through all the years to come. That "one thing" is, of course, to finish reading this book as soon as they can!

Chapter Three

Let the Bad Times Begin!

THE BAD TIME – the time when the backtalk is likely to start – usually begins when the grandchild is about five. That, according to the experts, is the age of choice. Before five, the child is just sort of experimenting with rude behaviors, to see what kind of effect they bring. After the child turns five, backtalk is deliberate, the result of a deliberate choice to make you feel badly.

Here are the forms
that early backtalking might take:

1. Putdown of a lovingly made gift. "This sweater is so lame, Grandmother! I mean, nobody wears stuff like this."

2. Sneering at a purchased gift. "Grandma, you got this at K-mart! I hope nobody I knows finds out."

3. Insulting a friend or relative. "Aunt Edna, that hairstyle looks like a wig!" Or worse, insulting you. "Grandmother, your house smells awful!"

4. Refusing to join activities. "I'm not going pumpkin picking this year! That's for little babies!"

5. Using words like "Stupid." As in, "That new wall paper (or shelf or landscaping or anything else you just purchased or had installed) is stupid, Grandfather."

6. Using a supercilious (okay, snotty) tone of voice that sets your nerves on edge.

7. Rolling her eyes at everything you say.

8. Saying "I don't think so!", "Give me a break!" and in other ways acting put upon at the slightest suggestion involving her participation, even those (such as playing the Dorothy game or making tissue paper flowers) she used to consider fun.

9. Pouting and sulking to get her way. These pouts and sulks can ruin anything, from a dinner out to an entire vacation.

10. Ignoring you completely. Refusing to respond is one of the most annoying, insulting forms of backtalk of all.

There are other forms of backtalk, but these are some of the most common. The main thing to remember is, *all* forms of backtalk are bad.

Why? Because A) they hurt, B) no grandparent deserves them, and C) they make the backtalkers mean. You do not want your grandchild to be a mean person.

How you respond to the first backtalk attack is so important. Your reaction teaches the backtalker the following:

1. Whether or not he can get what he wants from you by backtalking.
2. Whether or not you are going to put up with the backtalking.
3. Whether or not you think backtalking is okay.
4. Whether or not he should use respectful communication with you even if he doesn't have to practice it with anyone else.

How should you react? I'll get to that question soon. First, here are some ways you should not react.

Do not do the wrong thing.

Too many grandparents do the wrong thing when the backtalk occurs.

For example:
- They ignore it (which means it'll get worse).
- They get furious (which makes them look and feel like idiots – old idiots at that).
- They become self-pitying.

- They make excuses for the child. "He's tired." "She's overexcited." "She's been watching those awful movies again." "His parents are going through stressful times."

The right things to do:

The right things to do are to practice the following four steps. They are the same as those outlined in *Backtalk: Four Steps to Ending Rude Behavior in Kids*. According to parents I've spoken with, and those who've written reviews for the book on Amazon.com, these steps work like magic. I've been thanked for these steps over and over again, by people in all parts of the country, of all ages, in all kinds of family situations from blended to communal to nuclear, with kids from toddlers to teens. So grateful were some of them that I was often embarrassed.

The next chapter explains the four steps in detail.

Note: Adults are always modeling behaviors for children. So watch your own backtalk with friends and family when your grandchildren are watching. That affectionate putdown you use on your spouse and friend is seen by your grandkids as acceptable speech to be imitated.

Chapter Four

The Four Steps Reviewed

Step One is recognizing the backtalk.
THE BEST WAY to recognize it is to ask yourself, "Did it hurt?" But hurt, especially from one you adore, is not that easy to acknowledge. There sits your adorable nine-year-old grandson, the source of so much joy in the past nine years. He's just said "God, you're a dork!" when you asked if he wanted to play Parcheesi – always a favorite game for both of you. For good measure, he added "Parcheesi is so dumb!" with a lot of eye rolling and shaking of his head.

You are, admit it, stung. There is something in his tone that, for the first time since you've known him, is not cute. It's definitely not bantering, or even a challenging. It's a kind of cruel edge that is meant to demolish – to put down and insult. And it hurts!

You want to think:

"I'm overreacting."

"He didn't mean it."

"He ate too much sugar yesterday."

"I'm not used to the way kids talk today."

Why? Because thinking these things helps the hurt.

But the truth is, you have to hurt! You must feel what you feel, which is wounded, winged, zapped and zinged! If you don't feel your feelings, you'll sweep the backtalk under the rug, and set yourself up for getting backtalked again!

Step Two is deciding on a consequence for the backtalk.

I'll go into this step more thoroughly in a later chapter. But for now, understand that the best consequence to impose is refusing to do something for the child that he enjoys because his backtalk has taken your motivation away. You would not give a lovely gift to an adult who had just knowingly insulted you, would you? So, you will not go to Gymboree or any other favorite place with a child who has just insulted you – never mind that it's one of his favorite places to go.

The consequence teaches your grandchild a very simple rule: You can't make people feel awful and then expect them to want to be with you, or do something nice for you. Their parents, teachers and peers may not have taught them this rule, but you can!

Grandparents are in the perfect position to teach them this rule because, if they're typical, they do a *lot* of nice things for their grandkids that use up tons of energy, time and money. Any of these lovely things can be taken away as a consequence of backtalk – and *should* be!

**Step Three is enacting
the consequence for backtalk.**

You take this step by announcing what you are going to do, and why, and then following through. You say, "That kind of speech (or if gestures, communication) is unacceptable. As a result, I'm not taking you to the Dodgers game this afternoon." Now this may be huge. You may have paid hundreds of dollars for the best seats, you may have made an arrangement to introduce the grandchild to a player you know and the grandchild may have been looking forward to this event for months. It doesn't matter. All of these facts make this consequence a terrific way of showing you mean it. Rude talk is not acceptable. At all. Ever.

Yes, I'm softening a bit.

But I realize you may not be able to enact a consequence this huge. So, I'm going to do something for you grandparents I did not do for parents in *Backtalk:* let you start small. If you can't handle enacting a huge consequence, don't. Begin with the everyday treats – the movies, mall trips, repelling parlor visits, the local Olympic Swimming Pool outing. Little Jason or Tiffany should get the idea from your withholding of these routine benefits as consequences that backtalk is definitely not okay. I'll talk more about choosing and enacting consequences in chapters to come.

Step Four is ignoring (or disengaging from) the grandchild's protest.

Step Four is ignoring the grandchild's protest that he displays when he realizes you, the person who most adores him in the entire world, mean it. You are really going to enact this consequence.

This step takes lots of mental stamina, but will be so worth it in the long run. As time approaches to leave for the pool or the mall or wherever and you are not getting ready to go, he will probably get furious. He may try everything – bullying ("You better go to the pool today like always or I'm never coming over here again!"), supplicating ("Please, please, Grandma – I'll never be rude again!") and sadness (fighting back tears) – he can think of.

Too bad. You've disengaged. The matter is closed. The most you can say is, "Maybe another time," in a cheerful, matter-of-fact voice. And meanwhile, you go on to some other activity, that has nothing to do with the child.

Pretty soon, the child will give up trying to get you to see how mad he is and do something else.

It'll be hard on you, so hard. If you have any doubts about what you're doing, see *The Miracle Worker,* that film about Helen Keller starring Anne Bancroft and Patty Duke. It shows how teacher Annie Sullivan had only one hope of getting through to her deaf mute, totally spoiled charge: creating and enforcing consequences despite Helen's incredibly strong (often physically brutal) protests.

Remember: You will be doing your grandchild the biggest favor of his life!

All right, I know. You could never be so harsh. Life is too short. You don't need the kind of aggravation these steps will create.

Fine. But ask yourself: do you need the kind of emotional pain and subjugation the backtalk creates?

As I said before in this book and will again: if you don't do something to stop the backtalk when it starts, you'll be getting more of it. Do you deserve this kind of tyranny? After all you've done? After all the love you've lavished on this child? No. But then, no one deserves such treatment. These steps can take from a few days to weeks to be effective. Small investment considering the reward!

How about this: don't decide to implement the consequences in the book just yet. Just keep reading to the end, allowing the ideas to seep in. You can get mad at these ideas if you want, saying, "Me? Deny Chucky and Brittany anything their little hearts could desire? I could never do anything so extreme!"

But you may begin to see, by the time you're through, that the best gift and service you can ever give your grandchildren is teaching them that rudeness is not acceptable, ever, that their message can be communicated in other ways than by insulting. And you'll have a much better time with them as they grow into teens and then adults with children of their own!

The next four chapters elaborate on the Four Steps in more detail.

Chapter Five

Step One:
Recognize the Backtalk

The Story of Sarah

SARAH IS A 61-year-old grandmother of a 13-year-old, Jill, and her three brothers, 3, 5, and 7. Jill and Sarah have always been the best of friends, enjoying many kinds of activities together. Then one day, Jill said something that bothered Sarah. "She told me my whittled peasant figurines were 'too kitsch.'

"I said 'What do you mean, kitsch?'

"She said, 'you know, like old ladies decorate their houses with.' "

Thinking Jill was just misinformed, Sarah began telling her the story of how these figurines had been whittled by her great grandfather in Switzerland. "But Sarah just cut me off, announcing she wasn't interested. She said, 'Grandma, you should put these tacky things in the closet and buy some good stuff.'"

Like what, Sarah wanted to know.

"'Like, you know, dolls, those dolls you send for out of the newspaper. Susie's mom has 16 of them, all over her house. They're so adorable, you should see!'"

Sarah remarked coldly that such dolls did not suit her taste and let the matter drop – for then. "I didn't like that discussion with Jill. I did not like the tone of voice she used or her choice of words at all. But I figured she was just expressing her opinion. When I told Jill's mom, my daughter-in-law, about this incident, she said all kids acted like that these days and that I was overreacting. My son, her father, said I was overreacting. So," Sarah added with a shrug, "there you are. What could I do? I decided I was overreacting and let it go."

But the incidents with Jill kept happening. Whatever Sarah did, wore, and said was now put down snidely by Jill, often in front of her brothers and friends.

At the weekend sleepovers Sarah often hosted for Jill and her friends, the put-downs became especially frequent. The other guests soon began copying Jill's disrespectful attitude, making the sleepovers quite unpleasant for this grandmother. "I'd look forward to these events and buy the drinks and send out for pizzas and get my house cleaned beforehand. But after the kids had been at my house just ten minutes, I'd be miserable. Everything would be put down, my hairstyle, my new dress, you name it. First, one of them would look at me and say in this odd tone, 'Um, Sarah – 'I let them call me Sarah, 'where'd you get those earrings?' I'd tell her where, then say, 'why do you ask?' This child, this guest in my home, this consumer of my home-baked cookies, would look at the other guests and start giggling in this mean way. Then they'd all start giggling like they were making fun of my earrings. And they were! It became quite a game."

How did Sarah feel then? "Ashamed of my earrings! What did you expect!"

Obviously, Sarah was willing to do anything (she even sent for three Franklin Mint dolls, just to please Jill) except the one thing she needed most to do: Recognize Jill's behavior for the backtalk it was.

I'll get back to Sarah's story in the next chapter. Now, on to the best and easiest ways to identify backtalk as rudeness when your adored grandchildren inflict it on you.

How to recognize backtalk.

It may never happen to you, that first backtalk incident. Your relationship with your grandkids could go on being idyllic for the rest of your life.

But chances are very good that it will happen to you, and you need to be prepared.

Your first instinct will be to excuse it, justify it and call it by any other name. Here are a few of those justifications, excuses and euphemisms I picked up from grandparents I talked with:

- Inherited crankiness and whinyness ("Ronnie's mother always acted the same exact way when she was little!").
- Overtiredness.
- Homesickness.
- Being with those rude kids at school too much.
- Imitating the new stepfather (or mother).
- Starting on Ritalin.
- Stopping Ritalin.
- Starting in a new school.
- Not getting along with her new teacher.
- Not getting enough attention because both parents work.
- Getting too much attention because one parent does not work.

Such labels are your way of avoiding the truth. And the truth will be, you will feel hurt, unjustly attacked and mistreated. You'll be right to feel that way. No one deserves backtalk less than you!

Too many grandparents hate this moment so much they say it never happened. They talk themselves into believing that:

- Jason didn't mean it.
- Tiffy didn't know what she was saying.
- Brittany had no idea how that tone sounded.
- Jennifer watches too many television shows featuring sassy characters.
- Griffin plays too many of those videotapes starring harsh-talking heroes.
- Jason, Tiffy, Brittany and Griffin are just acting like they do at home so there's nothing anyone can do.

The grandparents may be right, all these things may be true.

But listen closely!

No matter what the reason for it, rude behavior is still rude. It still hurts.

And you don't want your darling grandchildren, who are otherwise perfect in all ways, to think rude behavior is okay.

Forms of backtalk

Backtalk is not just the zinging "You are so stupid, such a dork" type insult.

It can also be the rolled eyes, the head shaking in disgust, the expression of complete disdain and the Wendy and/or Wally Whiner tone that drowns your reasoned response, i.e. "You never let us stay at the pool (or the arcade or the riding stable) long enough! You only care about yourself!" or "I'm asking you a simple question, Grandma! God!"

One way to recognize backtalk is to ask yourself this question:

"Would I have been allowed to talk that way to my mom or dad?"

Chances are the answer is "No." But even if the answer is "Yes" (you might have come from a bohemian-type family that encouraged complete free expression or one that just didn't care), you don't have to put up with it from your grandchildren.

You should not put up with it – for their sake, if not yours. Not if you want them to be good parents and happy in their careers!

Avoid confusing backtalk with other forms of communication

How to distinguish between disagreement and backtalk:

Disagreement is delivered in rational, respectful tones. "Grandmother, I don't think the way you dry your dishes is necessary. It takes too long!"

Disagreement usually inspires discussions, not pain. "Really?" you may find yourself replying. "My own mother always took a long time to dry her dishes. I had to polish every dish, one at a time, and put it away."

To which your grandchild may reply, "I read in school that it's more sanitary to let dishes drain dry because the dish towel has germs. A girl won a science fair with that experiment."

To which you reply, "My goodness, Timmy. That's a convincing argument if ever I heard one. I'll try letting the dishes drain dry after dinner!" End of productive discussion.

As this exchange shows, disagreement is accomplished in calm voices. No yelling, overpowering, or temper tantrumming needs to take place.

How to distinguish between honest expression of the child's opinions and backtalk:

Honest opinions can be as painful as backtalk. But if honest opinions are delivered calmly and with honesty, they cannot be considered backtalk. For instance:

- "Grandpa, I don't like it when you yell at my mom on the phone."
- "Grandma, I hate it when you go next door to borrow something from Mrs. Rachet and don't come back for two hours."
- "Grandmother and Grandfather, I want you to stop getting in arguments when we're in the car. It makes me sick to my stomach."

- "Grandmother, I wish you wouldn't make me go to bed at 7:30 anymore. I'm allowed to stay up til 9 at home!"

These opinions might not be fun for you to hear, but they are honest forms of communication. Listen to them because they'll help you understand your grandchild a lot better!

Now, on to ways of stopping the backtalk that work – but might be more than a little scary to try at first.

Chapter Six

Step Two:
Choosing a Consequence
for the Backtalk

Sarah's Story, continued

WHEN LAST WE left Sarah, her 13-year old granddaughter, Jill, had been backtalking her mercilessly, not just when she was alone with Sarah in front of her friends, little brothers, and anyone else who happened to be around. Nothing Sarah did was safe from Jill's scathing backtalk.

Despite her daughter-in-law and son's opinion that Sarah was overreacting, Sarah had decided that Jill's communications hurt her and had to be stopped. "It got so I didn't even want to see Jill anymore and that was crazy, I loved her with all my heart!" Sarah recalls of that time. "She had been my first grandchild, the light of my life!"

How could Sarah stop the backtalk? As Sarah's friend, I recommended that she reread the *Backtalk* book (she had read it through once when it was first published, back in the days when her granddaughter was still an angel child, as a favor to me) and start implementing the Four Steps.

She did reread it and decided the first step had already been accomplished. She had admitted that Jill's treatment of her was backtalk. The time had come, she decided, to go on to Step Two and decide what the consequence of Jill's backtalk would be.

Was it easy for Sarah to arrive at this point? It certainly was not. Sarah is a widow, and her children and grandchildren are her life. To risk that close relationship was frightening indeed. But to allow it to continue at the expense of her self-respect did not appeal to Sarah, either.

The consequence was actually easy for Sarah to arrive at. She does things for Jill every day, taking her to the mall to meet friends, having her over for dinner, taking her and some friends to the Japanese "fire restaurant," as her youngest grandson calls it, ordering out for pizzas if Jill is hungry when she's visiting. The next time Jill backtalked her, Sarah decided, she would simply withhold one of these activities from Jill.

Since Sarah did favors for Jill almost every day, she knew she could easily choose the favor to withhold. It would be the favor scheduled immediately after the backtalk.

As it turned out, Jill was rude to her grandmother on a Thursday. "I was helping her with her math," Sarah remembered.

"When I said I could not do a particularly hard problem – math is not my forte – Jill went into a snit. She called me stupid. She rolled her eyes. She said, 'I don't know why I even ask you to help me, Grandma!' I'd been trying to help her for the past two hours. I could have been eating Japanese with a friend – something I love doing, but I thought Jill needed the homework help – and I did not deserve that kind of treatment."

The next planned favor for Jill was a sleepover for her and her brothers the following evening. It had been arranged so that the parents could go off on a weekend getaway.

"Jill, that kind of talk is not acceptable. As a result, you find somewhere else to stay tomorrow night. I'm not having you here."

"Come on, Grandma," Jill said, "give me a break. You know you don't mean that. We always do pizza on Fridays!"

Without replying, Sarah picked up the phone, and, as Jill watched, called Jill's home. When her son answered the phone, Sarah said that she had changed her mind, the weekend visit was off. "Sarah has behaved rudely and I will not have her over here."

"Come on, Mom," her son said, "you know you don't mean that. We have reservations at Del Coronado, for gosh sakes!"

"The boys can come over. But you better make arrangements for Jill somewhere else."

After a quick good-bye, Sarah hung up the phone. Jill was looking at her with eyes brimming with tears.

To be continued in the next chapter...

The important requirements of a good, effective consequence:

The consequence should be expressible in one or two calmly worded sentences. "That kind of talk is not acceptable. As a result, I will not be taking you to Toyland this afternoon."

The consequence should, ideally, be enactable within 24 hours after the backtalk occurs. If you must wait longer, remember: You'll need a lot of self discipline to enforce it because:

A. Your grandchild will have had that much longer to get you to change your mind about enacting it.

B. Your memory of how you felt will have dissipated and you just won't feel as strongly about enacting the consequence anymore.

The consequence should involve one incident only:

The consequence should spare you expense, energy, time and effort you were planning to expend on the grandchild.

The consequence should involve denying something the grandchild wanted, and/or was looking forward to and/or (even better) had come to take for granted, such as getting to watch movies at the multiplex every Saturday.

What to avoid in choosing a consequence:

- Anything that is ongoing, such as being grounded for any length of time.
- Anything that has to wait longer than five days, such as not taking a trip scheduled for the following week.
- Anything that the child might not want, anyhow. Not going to visit dear Aunt Clara that evening might be just what the backtalker wanted! Not getting her hair permed, not going shopping for his new high-top shoes, any of these could be secretly desired by your darling. You must keep a close eye on what they really like! *Don't think that getting up and going home every time your grandchild acts up in a restaurant is necessarily choosing and enacting a consequence the child might not want. Lots of kids would love leaving the stuffy, formal atmosphere of a restaurant to go anywhere else. The only people this consequence affects badly will be you and the other adults who were looking forward to eating out!*

- Anything that might really damage the child such as:
  A. Physical punishment.
  B. Yelling insults at the child (as in "You have a terrible mouth on you!").
  C. Attributing destructive motives (as in "You're always trying to ruin everything!" and "You want to make life miserable for everyone!") to the child.

The idea to remember is this:

You provide wonderful experiences for this grandchild and you deserve to be respected at all times. If you are not treated respectfully by this child, you can (and should) cut back on some of the wonderful experiences. Grandparents should never have to be emotional punching bags. Just because they spoil the grandchild need not mean the grandchild has to be a brat!

The truth about big consequences:

A big consequence is something like denial of a huge event. It's something that:
- Has been planned for a long time.
- Will probably cost a lot of money.
- May involve other people, too.
- Could provide the child with lifelong memories and education.
- Is often something you've been looking forward to, also.

Examples of big consequences include:
- Not taking a long-planned trip.
- Canceling plans for the child to attend a special camp.
- Not adopting a new pet.
- Not allowing the child to go with you to the big game.

If you enact any of these, be prepared: It will be hard. You will suffer. The child may be in too much shock to cry. You'll feel like reneging every five minutes. The child may decide to go home immediately. The parents may be mad at you.

Hopefully, you won't need to choose these big consequences. Smaller ones will do just as well. But if the smaller ones don't work, big consequences must be chosen and enacted. Rest assured they will work, if you can survive it. Why? Because, after a big consequence, the child will know once and for all that backtalk is not acceptable with you ever, at any time.

When to choose the most serious consequence of all:

What is it? Right – *sending the child home.*

A grandmother I know said this consequence works as well with the grandchildren's parents as it did her grandchildren.

"My grandson had arrived to visit me for a week while his parents were enjoying some much needed private time to themselves. He had just turned ten. I had not seen him in almost a year and found that he was terribly rude. Not knowing what else to do, I put up with the rudeness and backtalk, hoping it would stop." Seeing the child's treatment of this woman, a horrified neighbor gave this woman a copy of *Backtalk*. "By the time I read it, I knew what I wanted to do as a consequence." She called the parents on their cell phone and told them the boy's behavior was not acceptable, that she was putting him on a plane for home, and maybe she could try the visit again the following year.

"Then I hung up, told the child his backtalk was not acceptable, and as a result he was returning home. I would help him pack."

The boy's visit and the parents' private time was cut short by six days.

But when the boy visited this grandmother the following year, he was polite and respectful the entire time. "My son-in-law and daughter had finally taken the time to teach him what respectful behavior was – which they had needed to do for a long, long time!"

The best part of this consequence was, their grandmother said, that it kept her from having to get mad. "I didn't have to raise my voice. Everyone concerned already knew the next year that if he backtalked he would be immediately sent home – because I'd already done that the year before!"

This case history shows how effective this consequence can be. But you must make sure ahead of time that:

- The parents are not going away on a trip to an inaccessible place while the child is visiting.
- The parents will always be accessible by cell phone during the child's visit.
- You can afford any change in transportation price this consequence might require.

Note to remember
about choosing a consequence:

I've said this elsewhere, but I'm going to repeat it here:

You have to make lists of all the things you do for your grandchild. Yes, actual lists. I suggest finding or creating a huge calendar on which you can list your treats and services for the coming month, or as far into the future as you can. As soon as you think of another delight, write it down on the appropriate day with the time frame it will take. (Say, "The petting zoo 1 to 4 p.m.) If you don't make a schedule, you will have trouble thinking up a consequence and that will make you seem indecisive.

When you finish your schedule, you can relax. The next time you need a consequence, you take a quick look at your calendar and there it is – not driving your grandchild to a friend's birthday party that day. Not going to the Pandemonium Pizza Palace for lunch and bumper car riding.

You won't have to think twice.

As one father of three told me after reading *Backtalk*, "The four steps work wonderfully – if I can just think up a consequence when I need it! That's the hardest part about using your book."

Chapter Seven

Step Three:
Enacting
the Consequence

Sarah's Story, continued

WHEN LAST WE saw Sarah, she had just informed her granddaughter Jill and her son and daughter in-law that, because of Jill's backtalk, she would not be having Jill over that weekend. Jill was in tears. Yes, Jill's three little brothers could come over, but not Jill. Jill's parents were going away that weekend and Jill would have to find somewhere else to stay.

It was now time to enact the consequence Sarah had announced.

"Easy? Are you kidding?" Sarah said. "Enacting that consequence was no fun. They all kept trying to get me to change my mind. My daughter-in-law was especially persistent, saying it was too short notice to find Jill another place to stay, so if I'd take her just this once I'd never have to baby-sit her again."

"But I didn't give in," Sarah continued. "I knew if I did, I was dead. I'd taken my stand, and now I had to follow through."

She did follow through. "What happened was, nobody came over to stay with me because the parents decided not to go away that weekend."

Guilty? "Of course they tried to make me feel guilty. But you know what? The harder they tried, the less guilty I felt."

Did she miss her grandchildren that weekend?

"I tried to keep busy with shopping, and playing bridge and nursing home visiting."

Step Three,
enacting the consequence, requires:

1. An announcement of the consequence, along with the reason for enacting it. "That kind of talk is not acceptable. As a result, I am not taking you to the roller rink this afternoon." The tone should be absolutely calm, but pleasantly firm.

   Note: An announcement is not a threat. A consequence is not negotiable. Hence, no "if" words are allowed, as in "If you call me that word one more time, no roller rink for you today."

2. An enactment of the consequence. In this case, it is not driving to the roller rink. "Easy!" you say. "Piece of cake! What's so hard about not doing something?" You forget:

A. How persuasive a determined preteen or teenage child can be! Or how angry she can get! Or, as can be seen in Grandmother Sarah's case, the grandchild's parents!

B. That your whole schedule may have to be rearranged. If you don't go to the roller rink, you won't be going near the tearoom, where you planned to meet your friend for latte and scones while your grandchild was at the skating rink. Or you won't be going to the hairdressers for the wash and set you had scheduled. You get the idea.

3. Cancellation of any plans made that are affected by this consequence. That means calling to cancel reservations at the rink, and informing parents of other children you were taking or going to meet there that Jason will not be at the rink this afternoon. No, you don't tell these people what happened, you just say, "It's not going to be possible," and perhaps offer hope for "next time" whenever that might be.

But, as Henry Ford advised, you should never complain or explain.

Note: When the backtalk is attached to bad behavior, concentrate on the backtalk instead of the behavior. Studies have shown that once the backtalk is handled, the unwanted behavior also stops.

Chapter Eight

Step Four:
Disengage
from the Protest

Sarah's Story, concluded

SARAH'S FAMILY, HER daughter-in-law, her son and her grandchildren, began protesting the enactment of her consequence the very next day.

How could she be so insensitive? So uncaring? So selfish? Didn't she realize her granddaughter was only kidding when she talked back? And, most of all, when was she going to get over this snit and baby-sit granddaughter Jill again?

"It was hard!" Sarah recalls of that protest time, shaking her head. "Every time I answered the phone it was Jill or my son or my daughter-in-law telling me they needed me to baby-sit Jill and expected me to say of course, I'd do it.

"But you know what? I said, 'I'm not babysitting Jill anymore. I thought I made that clear.'

"So then they'd beg. 'Just this once. She'll act right. She promises.'"

Then, after about a month, Sarah woke up one day and decided she'd try babysitting Jill again. "If she behaved right." Which meant "No backtalk. At all!" from Jill.

To make a long story short, Sarah and Jill are now the closest grandmother and granddaughter anyone would want to see. Jill's friends and Jill behave respectfully – to Sarah, anyway. They all have sleepovers and pizza dinners and outings together just as happy families are supposed to do. All because Sarah used the Four Steps to stopping backtalk.

And she used Step Four (ignoring, and disengaging from, the protest) exactly the way it should be used.

Why Step Four can be difficult:

When Tiffy sees you mean it, that you will not take her skating, that you are going to enact a consequence, she will:

- Beg for a second chance.
- Have a tantrum.
- Try to negotiate. "Just let's go skating today and I won't ask to go the rest of the summer." Or, "Take me skating just this once and I'll wash and dry all the dishes for the rest of my visit."
- Threaten you. "If we don't go skating today, I'm going home right now." Or, "I'm

calling my mom. She'll never let you get away with this!"
- Sob piteously.

Your only response can be to ignore all the above attempts to protest your decision and get you to change your mind.

Here are some rules to remember:
- Try not to leave the child alone where you cannot see what she's doing. In *Backtalk*, parents were urged to go anywhere but where the child was protesting, but this advice has since struck me and others whose opinion I respect, to be a bit too risky to recommend. Never having been thwarted at all in their entire lives, some kids get so angry when they realize (often for the first time) they will not be getting their way, they can get quickly out of control.
- Remaining with them does not mean engaging with them. Sit in a chair in the same room, but try not to pay attention to them at all. Read, write letters, dust plant leaves, do anything to show that you've moved on to a new topic mentally, whether the child has or not.

Note: When disengaging from the child's protest, do not call someone on the phone.

You want to make the child feel as though the consequence is non-negotiable, not as though he himself is being rejected completely in favor of someone else.

· If the child calms down enough and appears to be making an effort to accept the consequence, offer this hope: "Maybe we can try skating again tomorrow." If the child begs for a firm commitment to take him skating, shrug your shoulders and say, "It depends. We'll see."

The child will know exactly what you mean, that the skating depends on whether or not he backtalks again. You won't have to, and should not, say another word. By that time, hopefully, it will be time to go to the store or fix dinner or welcome the other grandparent home from somewhere, and to consider the entire backtalk incident finished.

This is the end of Part I, the Four Steps you need to know to deal with backtalk in grandchildren. Coming up in Part II are 16 more ways to stop kids' rudeness from ruining your precious relationship with them. Some of these ways reiterate and elaborate on the Four Steps, but as I've heard from readers, these steps cannot be repeated often enough. Even then, they need to be gone over again and again to keep the backtalker from getting the upper hand in the home!

PART II

Sixteen Ways
to Keep Rudeness from Ruining
the Grandparent-Grandchild
Relationship

Chapter Nine

Treat Your Grandchildren Better Than You Did Your Children

WHAT PARENT, REALLY, has time to treat his or her children well?

There are too many things to do, such as make sure they're fed, clothed and housed, entered in the right play groups, enabled to pursue the sport of their choice, accepted into the right preschool, kindergarten and other schools, affiliated with the best SAT test tutor, and taken to all the enrichment lessons enjoyed by their peers. It all takes a lot of rushing them from pillar to post, making sure they practice the lessons and sports and do the homework and attend the tutoring sessions, and none of it is, let's face it, often very much fun. But the point of all this effort is to produce happy, healthy, accomplished young adults who will marry well and produce the grandchildren who will teach you what happiness really is.

The grandchildren are the ones you have fun with. Here are some things to do with those grandchildren that you may not have had time to do with your kids.

- Take them on excursions to places of local interest that you may like, such as museums, historic sites, and elaborate churches filled with wonderful music and statues of the saints. Then tell them stories about the paintings and the famous battles and architectural wonders and lives of the saints that will make them love these places, too.
- Pursue activities they'll like but you may not.
- The roller rink, the miniature golf course, the bumper and racing car parlor, the movies and the mall are fine.
- Talk to them all the time about everything.
- Listen to the things they say. Mom and Dad may ask them how they're doing in school, but do they actually take the time to listen to what's said? Did you always listen to your children? Not likely.
- Tell them how much money you planned to spend on them in a given period of time, and let them decide what they want to buy with it. Drive them around till you find the best deal on whatever it is.

Do not, if you can help it:
- Give them lots of sweets. Nothing can ruin a child's mood faster than sugar. *(More on that topic in a later chapter.)*

- Make them sit quietly while you visit with other adults. You're supposed to be having fun with them, not denying them your attention!
- Make the grandkids your only interest in life. Yes, make them the focus of your attention when you're with them. But they need to know you have other interests in life besides them. This topic is so important I've devoted the next chapter to it entirely.

Chapter Ten

Get a Life: Another Life
Besides the One You Devote
to Your Grandchildren

NOTHING MAKES PEOPLE act rudely toward you more than the knowledge they're it, they're all you've got, so they can be in any mood with you they want and treat you according to their whim. And there's nothing you can do about it.

A woman I know named Moira said she didn't mind being a divorcee in her retirement years because she had her four grandchildren to care about. And care about them she did – always ready to baby-sit at a moment's notice, have them for any and all meals, pick them up and take to their many lessons and sports and friends' homes, and appointments with doctors, dentists, orthopedists, and dermatologists – the older two had acne that would not clear up. Mom and Dad hardly had to do anything but give Grandma a call, and she'd come take care of anything anyone needed at any time. So what if the kids treated her rudely, speaking to her often as if she were an old, unappreciated family servant. They accepted her offers of dinners at pizza places and movies and trips to the toy store to buy whatever they wanted. Didn't that mean they really loved her more than they showed?

"Moira," said her worried friends, "Be careful. You're putting all your eggs in one basket."

"Four baskets," Moira would say proudly. "I'm impartial!"

"And one day you'll be sorry."

"Never," said Moira. "I'm doing exactly what I wanted to be doing at my age and I don't need anything or anyone else in life."

One day, Moira's grandchildren were invited to spend an entire summer with relatives 3,000 miles away. "They'll never go," Moira said to her friends. "They couldn't leave me that long."

But they did go. And Moira almost died. Literally, she nearly died from pneumonia she allowed to progress to the fatal stage because she was too lonely for her grandchildren to notice that she had become very ill. One day, a friend with a key to Moira's apartment found Moira near death and got her the medical care that saved her life.

After recovering from her pneumonia, Moira realized, with the help of her doctor, that she was depressed. This doctor referred Moira to a counselor, who was able to help

Moira get some medication for the depression and work through her fear that there was no other life for her besides her grandchildren.

After a few weeks of treatment, Moira found a part-time job, got deeply involved in tole painting (something she'd always wanted to do) and took up volunteer work with homeless high school students. By the time the grandchildren came back, Moira was immersed in many activities that, instead of distancing her from the kids, made her all the more interesting to them. Today, they proudly display her tole painting trays to visitors and the oldest has taken up this art herself. All four participate in her fund-raising activities for the homeless high schoolers. The four of them got the idea of initiating "personal hygiene product drives" for this population, going door to door collecting unopened bottles of perfume, shampoo, skin lotion and makeup samples that the homeless high schoolers were very happy to get.

Moira was also now less willing to put up with rude behavior from her grandchildren, and more able to say no when their demands were outrageous. (i.e. "Grandma, I'm bored – let's go to the movies and Pizza Hut, and then I want you to buy me the new Barbie I just saw on TV.") She was also able to require her grandchildren's parents to contribute financial help when they asked her to take the children to a movie or to order them take-out food when she baby-sat at their house.

To sum up – you really have to have your own life in your grandparent years, a life apart from your grandchildren that satisfies you – if you are going to have a good life with them.

Chapter Eleven

Set Your Own Rules

IT'S ALL RIGHT to have your own rules. You don't have to be dictatorial about these rules but you can have them. And you should have them. If children think people are going to live by *their* rules all the time, they'll never learn to respect anyone.

Note: Any rude ridiculing of your rules by your grandchildren can be classified as bona fide backtalk.

You can set rules about bedtimes, cleaning up after meals, leaving muddy shoes in the hallway, even forbidding certain videotapes in your house. You can set daily routines, activities agendas ("Tonight, we're watching this video I rented about these two children with disabilities who helped each other."), length of telephone calls and kinds of food that is eaten ("We have pizza once a week. I bought you pizza five times this month. I'm making meatloaf tonight. You will love it!") when you're with them.

If your rules are too strict, you'll know it. Not from backtalk, but from a stony kind of silence, or sad kind of sighing submissiveness and/or withdrawal of communication. In these cases, you can consider lightening up on your rules. Maybe the dinner dishes *can* wait until after *The Science Guy* on PBS, or you might consider that your tone of voice is a bit too stern.

Just so you never lighten up on your backtalk-consequence enactment.

Note: Remember! Your grandchildren need *a grandparent who enforces healthy, firm rules. Children have too few rules to follow today. It used to be that children adjusted themselves to the rules of adults. Now, in our country, it's the other way around.*

Chapter Twelve

Set Your Own Standards

LAST YEAR WHEN your grandson and granddaughter visited, they were models of perfect children, little sweeties who spread joy and good manners wherever you took them.

This year, mini rap-group singers get off the plane, hair spiked in greasy neon yellow, blue and/or pink stalks, bodies pierced in unlikely places and, in the girl's case, showing as much of a bare tummy (the flatness of which, you will discover later, has required her to become practically anorexic) as she can without her tiny skirt falling off, and as much of her maturing bust as the law will allow. (She's already told Mom and Dad she wants a breast augmentation operation for her birthday with just a little lipo on her "disgustingly huge" hips thrown in.) When you ask her to put on a shirt, she slips on a tight tee that has "69" printed in large figures on the front and a wide open female mouth on the back. ("No," she says, she doesn't know what "69" stands for, but it's seen on shirts worn by all her school chums.) All too often, conversation has sexual and violent connotations that you pray they don't really understand.

"Wait!" you tell me. "Kids don't act like that today. You exaggerate!"

Alas. The description above is not exaggerated. As of this writing, the look described is *de rigeur* in junior high schools; the sale of sexually explicit t-shirts is booming in mall boutiques. What are you going to do? Realize this: You probably can't do anything right away. But do not make the following mistake:

The mistake most grandparents make:

They start criticizing right off the bat. "You look awful! You can't talk like that! I won't tolerate pierced flesh in my house!"

That kind of behavior makes kids rude in return. It's too judgmental!

Instead, try saying, "How interesting you look! So different from last year!"

Get the grandchildren to tell you why they dress the way they do (are friends influencing their fashion choices? MTV, perhaps?) What it was like to get pierced? Did it hurt? And how on earth did they ever find a hair gel strong enough to get those spikes to stand up like that?

Later, you can let them know you're uncomfortable with the way they look and would like them to be more conservative while they're visiting. It's no big deal, you can add. It's just that you have different standards than their mom and dad and teachers and friends.

"Oh, come on, Grandma," they'll say in so many words, "you can't have standards we don't like. You love us unconditionally!"

"Yes," you can reply sweetly. "But I still have my own standards."

Decide right now how much:

- bare midriff flesh,
- cleavage,
- talk of sex,
- sexual language on clothes,
- talk of violence,
- new body piercings

you will tolerate on an extended visit from the grandchild.

Here's the best way to announce your standards to the child. "Darling," you can say in a gentle but firm tone, "I'm not comfortable with skirts that tight and the tops that low and all that bare tummy showing. Let's go shopping for clothes you'll like that I can live with."

A rude response to this kind of fair, reasonable statement should be treated as backtalk.

You must at least establish a tolerable compromise. This compromise shows you still intend to enforce your standards, but in a reasonable way.

Chapter Thirteen

Do Some Research

IT OCCURRED TO an academic colleague and me a year or so ago that everyone in the educational field was making judgments of teachers today without talking to any of them. Research methods consisted of sending out thousands and thousands of surveys asking teachers their opinions and then judging them by the small percent of the surveys returned.

My colleague and I wanted to find out how teachers felt students had changed in the last five years. Instead of sending out surveys, we took 46 teachers in seven states to dinner. During these dinners, we found out all the ways students had changed that were affecting the lives of teachers. For instance:

Kids want to use media – TV, videogames, music and the Internet – all the time, even in the classroom and during all social occasions where they might be the least bit bored. (At a dinner party I attended recently, a mother had to tell her teenaged son to remove his earphones and make an effort to participate in the conversation going on.) Kids can only absorb lessons in short soundbites. Kids have little parental guidance anymore, thanks to divorce, shared custody, both parents working and parents seeing kids more as peers than as children.

My colleague and I came away from this research project with a much better idea of what today's children are like and why. We no longer have to be shocked at the way kids are dressing and speaking and piercing their flesh. They are just doing what their media idols do and media idols are more influence on kids these days than anyone else.

Take a teacher out to eat.

Before criticizing anything your grandchildren do, take a teacher to dinner (they seldom have time for lunch, even on weekends). Tell her, over the potato skins and grilled chicken (favorites with most of the teachers we took to dinner) that you want to know more about kids today so you can relate to your grandchildren better.

You'll find out:
A. What schools are like.
B. What the other children are like.
C. What the teachers are like.
D. What you can and cannot expect to change about kids today. You'll have developed an "informant" in the field, so to speak, who may serve as a resource when you

want to bridge the generation gap in years to come.

Other recommended research methods include reading teen magazines and *Rolling Stone,* attending at least two popular teen-oriented films, and watching a few episodes of one of those sitcoms featuring a bevy of teenaged stars. You may be shocked at all the sex and foul language and violence you see, but at least you'll be more informed than another grandparent who has no idea why today's kids are the way they are.

Chapter Fourteen

Don't Be
a Sugar Pusher!

L OTS OF CHILDREN get mean when they
eat sugar. Why this happens involves
lengthy scientific and medical reasons that I
won't go into here.

**Here's what happens
with a sugar-addict kid:**
She eats refined sugar and enjoys it, then
about an hour later (more or less time can go
by, depending on the child's metabolism)
discomfort ranging from discontentedness to
outright rage will ensue. Usually it's a temper
flare-up directed at the handiest human target.

Along with this anger attack comes a
craving for more sugar. The adult present is
usually only too happy to oblige; he'll do
anything to make the child her sunny self
again.

While eating the shake or cookies or other
sugary product, the child is, indeed, happy
again – but only for a short time. The second
"sugar crash" is usually worse than the first,
featuring backtalk that simply will not stop
and may actually be out of the child's control.

Will the Four Steps for handling backtalk work in such a situation? Yes, but they will not work easily – the child feels very hostile and has to exert a great effort to stop the hostile behavior.

I know, I have this reaction to sugar. So did everyone in my family. When my parents and brother and I were bored in the evenings, we would make and eat fudge and then deal with the subsequent "meanies" and cravings for more sugar by going to bed or going out for ice cream sundaes.

You think you don't give your grandchildren much sugar? Try adding it all up. Chances are, if you are typical, you'll find that:

- Your child's breakfast cereal or pastry is actually a sugar treat.
- Mid morning snacks consist of sugar-filled cookies and/or sugar filled drink.
- Lunch involves sugar in a drink or dessert.
- Afternoon treats are often sugary in some way.
- Dinner out usually includes a milkshake or soda and sugary dessert, or a fruit drink (mostly sugar) and cake and ice cream for dessert if eaten in.
- If it's the Christmas holidays, forget it. Your children will be eating sugary delights from morning until night. I know one grandmother who brings plates of

Christmas tree cookies up to their rooms while they're sleeping in the event they should want a treat if they happen to wake up.

My dear friend, Lynn Wiese Sneyd, says in her excellent book, *Holistic Parenting* (Keats, 2000) that "the sugar lows following sugar highs may result in hypoglycemia (a condition of low blood sugar that helps create the mean disposition). If this pattern repeats itself too often, diabetes can ensue."

But children should not be loaded with artificially sweetened treats, either. Sneyd says that artificial sweeteners have been found to cause jittery behavior and increased susceptibility to infection, among other unwanted symptoms.

A group of teachers we interviewed who teach in an upper-socioeconomic income bracket high school said their students tended to drink only bottled mineral water which they carried with them everywhere, and snack on health-food store granola bars. You might want to model such eating habits for your grandchildren, telling them frequently how much better such foods make one feel, look and act than the sugar snacks. Tough challenge, but worth the effort.

Chapter Fifteen

Model Peaceful Behavior

LET FAMILY FIGHTS rage around you. Let anger at world events swirl up within you. Let fury at conservatives (if you're a liberal) or liberals (if you're a conservative) make you protest with the shrillness of a harpy at political meetings.

Just don't let these feelings show to your children and grandchildren.

"Wait!" you cry. "You're asking me to repress my real feelings with my family? Suppress my true self?"

Yes, I am. And all because of a dear friend of mine I'll call Maude. Maude always did have strong opinions in all the years I've known her. She was also blessed with a trust fund from her father, an equally opinionated man who knew, beyond a doubt, that the right-wing Republicans knew everything and had no patience for anyone who did not agree. He taught Maude to be the same way, and gave her full control of his financial empire.

Alas, Maude's beautiful daughter married a man who, on his own, had become quite liberal over the years. When Maude's adored grandchildren were young, she was too besotted with them to care what her son-in-law thought. But as he became less inclined to accept Maude's opinions on world affairs, political leaders, partial birth abortions and poverty without expressing his own, he soon found himself in heated arguments with her.

Once Maude got started on a topic that angered her, she could not stop. She fully expected her son-in-law to realize this fact and stop inciting her by disagreeing with what she said. "He has to realize I have a temper," Maude would say to me when reporting on her visits, "and that I'm not about to hold it just because of him!"

What Maude's son-in-law eventually realized was that he did not want Maude returning to visit ever again. When Maude's daughter informed Maude of this fact in a telephone call, Maude told her to stand up to her husband and tell him her mother certainly could come to visit her grandchildren, anytime she wanted.

But the daughter said she felt the same way as her husband. "You just upset all of us too much when you're here, Mom. I'm sorry, but it's true."

Maude was, to put it mildly, devastated. She still is. "They expect me to be someone other than myself!" she told me, at the top of her lungs. "Is that right? I ask you, Audrey, is that fair?"

"Yes," I wanted to say to Maude, "it is. You're not yourself anymore, you're a grandmother and grandmothers have to act loving and nice – all the time, no matter how they feel inside. It's the role the grandchildren need them to play in life." But I did not want Maude's wrath directed at me.

Really, the nice, loving role is not such a bad role to play at all. Yes, it is often difficult to maintain, especially when all those about you are in turmoil for one reason or another. But it makes you a model of love and light and laughter. And that is a lovely kind of model to be.

Grandparents should be the part of a child's life that remains constantly, and unshakably, calm, happy and full of light.

Chapter Fifteen

Set a Budget

S O MANY GRANDPARENTS have told me their grandchildren expect them to have not just deep but bottomless pockets when it comes to spending money on them, that I knew a chapter on money was necessary.

I learned a lot of grandchildren's rude behavior is inspired by money. If Grandpa does not buy everybody the large popcorn at the movies, if Grandma does not take them to the expensive arcade with the very best games, if Grandma and Grandpa even dare to buy them a knock-off phonics reading game instead of the real "Hooked on Phonics," grandchildren will behave rudely and believe they have every right to do so. Any excuse on the grandparents' part, such as not having the money for the exact things these kids demand, may elicit backtalk *extraordinaire*.

"Don't give me that excuse!" one grandchild told his grandparents when they said they could not afford the expensive game arcade. "Your stock just split three for one! I saw it on CNBC!"

How to end grandchildren's money demands:

I am a big believer in allowing kids to participate in budgeting sessions. Every month or week you can have a meeting with the grandchildren, explaining all your expenses, your income, and the amount you can allocate to entertaining them. They can then decide ahead of time where the entertainment money will go and how much of it will be spent where and on what. If you have stocks and savings, tell them how much (well, maybe not entirely how much) you have and why liquid conversion every time the child wants something new is simply not a good idea.

Children are so smart these days, thanks to technology and prenatal nutrition. They love this kind of learning and planning. Why they are not made a part of it at a very young age is more than I can understand.

The popcorn solution

Buying children treats at the movies is supposed to be part of the movie going experience. Saying "No" to the huge bag of heavily buttered popcorn with a huge soda (both of which are usually refillable for free these days) is just not done when taking kids to a film.

But then one grandmother I know realized she was spending $20 extra on these snacks every week when she took her two grandchildren and their friends to the movies. "And then afterward they'd want to go somewhere for dessert and arcade games."

She then read *Backtalk* and figured out what she would do. "I just said 'no' to the popcorn and soda. Just plain 'no.'

"Today, they don't ask for movie snacks. We buy our tickets, go right to our seats, and the kids never complain."

Why? "Because the last time they were rude about wanting popcorn and drinks, I said 'Fine, I'm not taking you anywhere afterward, I'm taking you right home now.' And I did."

If you have little money to spend on your grandchildren:

Let them know you have little money. Do not try to keep up appearances, tell them the truth. Provide attention, and lots of praise.

Here are some ways to lavish love on them that costs very little money at all:

1. Buy children's books at the dollar store and have someone videotape you reading to them. They can always play the videotape and look at the book themselves after you've gone home.

2. Go on adventure walks. Make up stories about people who live in the houses you see. A good witch perhaps? A retired king and queen?

3. Have older kids help write the family history in letter form. Just get the facts and let yourself tell the story in letters. This is called an epistolary-type novel and it's great fun and easy to write.

4. Organize gifts-for-relatives projects. Have your grandchildren donate handprints, small photos of their faces, photos of all their favorite toys on a chair, or other items that show who they are. With the grandchildren's help, make these items into mobiles or art groupings or montages suitable for displaying and send them to relatives who may be out of the family loop. This will teach the grandchildren the value of family connectedness and the fun of making beloved art out of pretty much nothing at all.

You get the idea. You can think up lots of projects on your own, so can the grandchildren. Have fun.

*And if you have lots of money
to spend on the grandchildren.*

Please be judicious. Spoiled children are almost always rude children. Grandparents who spoil them are almost never visited by them in their old age. How do I know? The nursing home my mother lived in during her last years was full of such unvisited wealthy grandparents. A nurse told me these lonely residents almost always got big, lavish funerals after they died, but seldom any attention while they were still alive.

Chapter Sixteen

Don't
Play Favorites

BELIEVE IT OR not, I had to be reminded about this rule for grandparents.

In my family, people tend to have one child. I had just one, my brother had just one, and his son, my nephew, had just one. (True, my mother had two, but always said it was one more than she was actually able to handle.) And we made much of our only children, not needing any more to make us happy. As my brother's wife said when her son was six months old, "Another child would just intrude on my relationship with this little prince!" I knew exactly how she felt.

Then, what do you know, my son and daughter-in-law had a second child and I was not at all sure how to act. By that time, I was wild about my darling first grandchild, Maria and just could not fathom needing another. So, in my most irrational of grandmotherly minds, I decided the second child could be for all the other relatives; I would keep Maria for myself. That seemed fair, didn't it? It did to me.

My son actually had to remind me that I should ask how Gia was when I called, that I should also send Gia a present when I sent one to Maria and I should remember to speak to Gia on the phone. And when I visited, I should divide my time equally among them, not just play with Maria all the time, now and then giving Gia a few perfunctory smiles and waves.

Yes, I was playing favorites. I didn't mean to, but I was.

You could be playing favorites, too, without meaning any harm. Perhaps you are most compatible with one of your grandchildren, or most fond of that one because she reminds you of another beloved relative or even of you, when you were that age. Perhaps you like one grandchild's looks the best, or disposition, or loving ways. It's hard not to fall hardest for the child who sends you "I-love-you" letters all the time, forsaking other grandchildren who are not so sentimentally inclined.

Keep it up and I can almost guarantee they'll all be rude to you before long. The favorite will be rude because he'll think you'll let him get away with it and the others will be rude because they'll resent your devotion to your favorite.

What do you do?

You find out the unique and special qualities of every grandchild and enjoy them as individuals. That seemingly sullen boy may delight you with his paintings, done secretly in his closet where no one else can see and make fun of them. That cheerleading fanatic who so seldom even acknowledges your presence when you visit may astound you with her knowledge of physical fitness, and her ambitions to get a cheerleading scholarship to a really fine school.

You give everyone of them a separate outing with you by him or herself, at least once a week if you can manage it, and, if you live far away, at least once every visit. During these outings, you make the grandchild with you feel special and wonderful just as he or she is, for him or her innate self. You'll be amazed at what this investment of time and love brings you in a very short time. (No, I won't tell you. You'll find out on your own.)

Make yourself include them all, on an equal basis, every time you have anything to give, even if it is just your attention. Pretty soon you'll be impartial because you want to.

I reached that point, finally. The first time Gia sang "Albuquerque Turkey" to me on the phone with all the words, from memory, I knew there was another grandchild as special as the first, just different and unique in her own way. *Two* perfect grandchildren to love, imagine that!

It amounts to riches beyond my wildest dreams.

Chapter Seventeen

Get Physical!

CHILDREN WHO ARE physically engaged are a lot less likely to be rude – they are much more likely to have better dispositions than children who sit around all day.

One of the teacher groups I interviewed taught classes in a rigorous academic program within a large public high school. To stay in this program, students had to participate in track for three hours a day, regardless of their health, their prior experience in sports or their interest in track. So superior were these students emotionally to students who were not in this program that the teachers think all students in all schools should have the three-hour a day track requirement. "They are so much more calm and attentive and respectful in the classroom!" one teacher exclaimed, and all the others agreed.

Be known as the grandmother who gets the children into sports. Drive them to soccer or tennis or basketball. If you can't drive for some reason, encourage foot races, long walks and bike rides. Get them to compete against themselves while you hold a stopwatch, if they are not of ages to compete against one another. Cheer loudly from the sidelines, if you can't be active yourself.

If the foregoing sounds ridiculous to you, that just proves I'm right. We've gotten so far away from taking responsibility for our physical activity in this country that even suggesting may seem corny, even pretty absurd.

Think about the father of Venus and Serena Williams. He had his daughters hitting tennis balls into couch cushions with used racquets long before he could afford a proper tennis club for them to go to.

But the idea is not to raise champions. It's to keep your grandchildren physically fit. If you do, you'll be closer to them now. And you'll be thanked by them profusely in years to come.

PART III:

How to Have
a Rudeness-Free Home
that Your Grandchildren
Will Love Visiting

Part III

Introduction

HAVE YOU EVER been in homes where the emotional atmosphere was so pleasant that no one living in them or visiting them would even think of being rude?

By the same token, have you been in homes where the atmosphere was so hostile that rudeness was the only form of communication used? As one young boy said in a *Parade* magazine interview, he loved TV because characters were so nice to each other on the sitcoms, and never yelled at the kids, the way people did in his home.

Educational Psychologist Robert E. Calmes, EdD, has been examining the pleasant kind of home for over 20 years, trying to decide exactly what qualities they possess.

After analyzing thousands of research studies and interviewing many clients in his private practice, Dr. Calmes decided that six qualities exhibited by the adults in charge are the ones that contribute to making homes rudeness free: Consistency, Reinforcement, Empathy, Genuine Care and Concern, Modeling of Desired Behavior, and Love of Animals, Plants and Inanimate Objects.

All of these qualities, or characteristics, work together in the home to provide a productive, pleasant atmosphere in which rudeness is out of place. Grandparents can put them to especially good use, because they might use a lot of them already, without knowing it.

Every one of these components constitutes one of the 20 ways of preventing rudeness from ruining your relationship with your grandchildren, so every one will get its own chapter.

All six of these chapters will give examples and explanations of the way these qualities can best be used. The chapters also tell what happens to kids in homes where these qualities are not used.

Chapter Eighteen

Use Consistency
in Your Interactions
With Grandchildren

CONSISTENCY IS ONE of the most important characteristics of a beloved grandparent.

It means that the grandparents can be depended on to behave in the same way almost all the time. It means that their attitudes, disposition, and lovingness can be counted on to be there whenever the child is with them, but so can their rules and their standards. Believe me, the child loves that kind of structure.

My mother provided this kind of consistency to my son and my nephew when they were young. At Grandmother's house, they always knew what would happen – meals on time, trips to the hardware store with Grandpa (which they both loved), and walks in the Cape Cod woods, every single day. They also knew what they could not do, such as beg for things in stores, fail to put away their toys and bother Grandmother during one of her "sick tired" spells. "Are you just a little tired or are you 'Gosh-darn it' tired, Grandmother?" my son (then four) once asked my mother when she said she had to lay down for awhile. A "little" tired meant he could count on her to get up in a while to play, the "Gosh-darn-it" tiredness meant he would have to entertain himself in his room for a while or help Grandpa with artwork. (This strange fatigue that would make my mother cry out in frustration, "Gosh darn it, I'm tired!" every couple of days or so never was diagnosed, alas.) He knew that when she got up from her rest she'd be her usual self.

In a biography, Oprah Winfrey was said to have counted on her grandmother's consistent behavior to guide her through an unusually difficult and tumultuous childhood. Other celebrities have said the same thing.

I can, unfortunately, tell you what it was like to have grandmothers who were not consistent. It was depressing and unsettling and not conducive to behaving well.

A victim of what we now suspect was early onset Alzheimer's, my mother's mother was displaying inconsistent behavior by the time I was about three. One day she would be sweet and attentive, the next she was disapproving of anything I did. And the next day, she would not care what I did or said, as though I did not really exist. I think the querulous disapproving days were the worst. Grandfather tried mostly to keep her happy, and had little time for me.

At any rate, I would return from week-long visits with them feeling pretty awful and acting out these bad feelings by backtalking everyone. As for Daddy's mother, she had a stroke when I was very young and was incapable of consistency, with me or anyone else. On lucid days, she seemed sweet, but on bad days would be annoyed with everything I did. Finally, she moved to a nursing home far away and I never saw her again.

Dr. Calmes says that the following list includes all the different behaviors grandparents can use consistently with their grandchildren:

- *Consistency of mood.*
  Yes, you can have a bad mood occasionally, everyone can. Just don't let the grandchildren know it.
- *Consistency of standard setting.*
  You know what your standards are and you teach your grandchildren to help uphold them. One particularly important standard is respectful speech. Your grandchildren know they must speak respectfully in your house to you and one another.

- *Consistency of routine.*

  Going to bed early, getting up early, doing certain chores on certain days at certain times, all these routines give important structure to children's lives.

- *Consistency of social life.*

  The people with whom you allow your grandchildren to socialize when they are with you should meet your standards of decency and respectful speech.

- *Consistency of kindness and generosity.*

  You make personal gifts for far flung and/or incapacitated family members. You take presents to nursing home patients at regular intervals. You always buy coupon books from the Boys Chorus members and cookies from Girl Scouts. You show your grandchildren all the time that such acts make you feel connected to a larger community. You do other charitable acts on a regular basis.

- *Consistency of financial responsibility.*

  You can't say you can't afford something the grandchild wants on one day and then splurge and buy it another day. Not a good idea!

- *Consistency of positive attitude.*

  A good grandparent's attitude should be positive most of the time. That way, negative attitudes, such as those necessary

for implementing the backtalk consequence,
are much more powerful in their effect.

Chapter Nineteen

Modeling Behavior
You Expect your Grandchild
to Display

THIS STEP IN the Calmes' plan is easy. You simply act the way you want your grandchild to act. He sees you acting that way, he'll act that way too, most of the time. That's how modeling works.

So, you want Jason to be respectful, cheerful, polite and nice to you and others. You simply model these traits to Jason and others he sees you interact with. Then, when you tell him that backtalk is not acceptable, he'll know you're right. In your house, it is not acceptable because he never sees it done by anyone.

A word about mainstream media:

You can model desirable behavior with your grandchildren. But what about the videogames they play? By the time you read this, the current video game hero will be obsolete so I'm going to make one up, based on those I've observed in my research. I'll call him Marty the Mauling Mutant. Marty is the hero of about eight videogames, all of which your grandson owns or wants to own. In these games, the player becomes Marty and hunts down various enemies, human and non human (the latest is the giant cyber-physico cockroach from 500,000 years in the future, a huge roach that has the brain of a genius and the ability to go from cyber to physical matter in nanoseconds). Marty does not just kill his enemies, he mauls them first, like a lion or tiger does his prey. First he strips off the limbs, and then removes the internal organs, all while the victim is screaming in pain.

"No!" you cry. "My grandson would never ever play a game so awful." Ah, but he does and so do all his friends. Why? Because these games exist and are marketed to nice children such as your grandson. It's all just business as usual.

Statistics show that your granddaughter is not likely to play these games. Girls really do not like them. But girls watch and listen to stars in music videos who want, pursue and appear to have lots of sex. Here's a typical star type they adore: Let's call her Normandee. We'll say she's a former child entertainer who wanted, as do all female youngsters these days, to be a famous singer. So she changed her image into that of a nymphet, with sexuality oozing from every inch of her very much exposed body. Despite being prepubescent, she's now a sexual being; gyrating and narrowing her very made-up eyes as she sings lovingly into the suggestively held microphone. The problem is, young girls are capable of sexual feelings, well before puberty, and the expression of them is being modeled by Normandee.

If Normandee and Mauling Marty are okay models for your grandchildren in your opinion, fine. But if they are not, you have the right to keep them out of your house. You can't keep them out of the grandchildren's lives but you can say, "I do not like you interacting with such role models when you're with me, so please keep the games and music videos at home." Get your cable TV disconnected if all else fails, and your VCR made inoperable by anyone but you.

Provide substitute role models immediately. *Anne of Green Gables* is great for girls. Read your granddaughters the books and show them some of the mini-series made from the books. For boys, I'd suggest live individual coaches in a sport, if you can afford it, or decent-living sports players. Talk about these players, read stories to your grandson about their lives, and think of other activities showing you consider these players to be models of desired behavior. Your grandson may not know that teams depend on players who lead stable lives and keep themselves healthy, not the players who indulge in scandalous (literally), self-indulgent behavior.

Once when I was baby-sitting, I accidentally locked the baby I was sitting inside the house when I stepped outside to get a toy. Not knowing what else to do (this was way before cell phones) I went knocking on doors of neighboring homes. The second one was answered by a very large man who was eating lunch with a wife and two children. He rushed to my aid and, with brute physical strength, was able to pull the locked door open so I could get back to the baby I was sitting. I was told later this man was a member of a professional football team. I've since seen that he's about to retire from that team, after 15 distinguished, but unscandalous years. And he's still married to the same woman.

Here is what you need to remember about media models: Kids turn to them if they have no other options. Tell them that Normandee and Marty are not the images to emulate. Normandee and Marty may be fun to watch, they are not heroes. They're just stars, figments of publicity people's imaginations.

Trust me, your grandchildren will be glad to hear this news. Children cannot, smart as they seem to be these days, figure out such truths for themselves.

Parents just don't have time to explain such things these days, and are not sure they should. Parents no longer seem to know what children need to know. But grandparents can do this explaining. And in the process, they'll have the opportunity to seem quite knowledgeable and even cool.

Chapter Twenty

Reinforcement

REINFORCEMENT, SAYS DR. Calmes, is crucial to a rudeness free home because it helps children learn and appreciate the value of not being rude.

In Dr. Calmes' definition, reinforcement means making sure that children have:

- More praise than blame.
- More success than failure.
- More reward than punishment.

So, you avoid concentrating on the negatives, and make much of the positive behavior.

What I love about the four step-method for handling backtalk is, it prevents you from having to go on and on about the backtalk, but provides you an action way of dealing with it swiftly and surely.

The three reinforcement methods explained:

Here are elaborations of Dr. Calmes' three methods of reinforcing desirable behavior in children: (More praise than blame, more reward than punishment and more success than failure.)

When your grandchildren are with you, praise the behavior you like. "Chucky, I think you are very good at giving me your contrary opinion on something without giving me a hard time. That's a wonderful skill to develop."

Avoid blaming! What is blaming? It is the attribution of traits and desires to the child. "Chucky, you just want to disagree with everything I say! You won't ever admit I'm right! You are just plain mean!" The problem with these statements is that neither you nor anyone else has the right to decide what another person wants – you must ask that person. And no one has the right to tell another person what he is – that's labeling and it's inaccurate, as well as destructive.

Research shows that blaming destroys children's self esteem because it amounts to attacking their actual selves, as they are. How can anyone like a self that wants to be mean and disagreeable? He cannot, so he thinks of himself as bad and unlovable and consequently acts in unlovable ways or in ways that are too good, trying to get approval and love for his awful real self.

Reward the efforts the child makes even if he does not succeed. "Chucky, you are trying so hard to get that sink clean" or "you have been practicing so diligently to learn *Fur Elise*.

You will get my special hard work reward, an extra half hour of reading aloud tonight!" Who cares if the sink is still grimy in spots and *Fur Elise* is full of missed notes? It's the effort that you want to reward, and the dedication to the task. Don't reward too often, and certainly not every day. Every few days is fine, when you're especially impressed by the child's cheerful persistence.

As for punishment, there really should not be punishment, ever. Punishment too easily becomes vengeance and is almost always arbitrary. Imposing consequences for undesirable behavior is a more humane notion of teaching children what not to do.

Providing more success than failure for the child is fun. You do things with the child, such as tidy a room or wash up the dishes or prepare a salad that end successfully. In other words, you work with the child on doing the things you want her to learn to do, such as cleaning her room, making sure the outcome is regarded as a success. "There, Yvette. Finished! We were very successful in getting this room clean!" Then you have Yvette do the job herself and remark on every aspect of this job that was a success. You avoid having the child fail by refusing to label the result of any honest effort as failure.

Use reinforcing language:

Children of all ages love being spoken to by adults in formal, encouraging words. "That is very resourceful and self sufficient of you!" I would say to my child long before he knew the definition of those words. But he seemed to like the sound of them. And the meanings must have sunk in over the years because now, he is one of the most resourceful and self-sufficient people I know. "That effort is admirable!" "Your persistence is remarkable!" Or, as my darling grandchildren are told frequently by their mother, "Very good job, Maria! (Or Gia). Very, very good." And so on. Try to be specific, try to have an encouraging tone, and try to mean what you say.

Discouraging and disparaging words:

"You can't do anything right!" "You never finish a job. I always have to finish it for you!" "You make me sick!"

As you can see, such statements and rhetorical questions leave the child with few options. She can't reply, "Yes, I do too finish jobs," or "I don't want to make you sick," because she's afraid of getting in trouble. And, she fears, these words might really be true. Thus, such statements make her begin to dislike herself in a way that is very deep and subliminal.

Avoid them at all costs. If you do make a discouraging, disparaging comment to a child take it back. Say you did not mean it and are so sorry.

Here are some remarks you should never say when the child backtalks you: (I got most of them from radio talk show callers who said these were the sort of things their parents had said to them.)

- "I can't believe you said that!"
- "What did you say to me?"
- "Are you sassing (or backtalking or being smart with) me?"
- "Don't you ever use that tone of voice with me again!"
- "You talk like a hussy!"
- "You sound like a juvenile delinquent!"

Such statements are really saying to the child that he is intrinsically bad in various ways.

How much better for the child's self esteem to say, simply and calmly, "That kind of speech is unacceptable. As a result, I am not going to." This statement focuses on the speech, not the child's inherent badness, and prevents you from having to get visibly upset and out of control.

Chapter Twenty-One

Showing Empathy

THIS STRATEGY FOR creating a rudeness free home is especially important for teenaged grandchildren.

Being a child today is hard, but being a teenager is especially difficult. Here is a list of reasons why:

- There are more bullies than ever before.
- At least half of all teens, in case you didn't know, are having sex. They have the same problems with it – the same fears of betrayal, worries about performance, anxieties about birth control and now, worries (very justified no matter how "nice" the partner) about getting AIDS – that adults have.
- Teens who are not having sex are being pressured to have sex by partners whose love they want to keep, people they love but who make sex a condition of the relationship, and friends who "do it" and think they are uncool prudes for not doing it.
- At least half of all teens work 30 hours a week at jobs. They have to in order to

afford cars, sports fees, cool clothes and class trips. This is in addition to going to school (which really is just as rigorous as ever and getting more so, with the movement to raise standardized test scores) and being involved in at least one extracurricular activity, if not more.

• Many teens have no primary source of loving care. Back in the days when only one parent worked, the stay-at-home parent would be available for the teen all the time, and the teen would go out to participate in all kinds of activities besides school, knowing Mom (seldom Dad) was there at home, eager to talk, play board games and take walks with him, accompanied by a snack of freshly baked cookies and milk. This situation meant that the teen had layers of caring to count on. There were the primary layers of caring from Mom and then Dad at home, and secondary sources of caring from friends and teachers at school. Today, there is seldom anyone home to care for the teen during the day. Both parents are working full time, are exhausted when they get home, and the day care stops when the child enters high school.

Thus, too many teens today have to seek primary caring from teachers, friends, and often from parents of friends who are not employed. These people are hopefully responsible influences. But if they are not, where else is the teen going to go?

Furthermore:

Teens are often involved in divorce situations and their lingering effects. Remember the study of teachers I discussed in an earlier chapter? The study in which I asked teachers how students had changed most in the past five years? One of the biggest changes for teens was the growing number of shared custody arrangements. Children of divorce living in these arrangements must have two sets of all school materials, one for the father's house, one for the mom's. They must also have a complete set of clothes at each house, and learn to have complete sets of friends in each setting, plus adjust to different sets of rules, not to mention, in many cases, at least one new set of step siblings and often two to get along with. Children get to see parents they've just lost being especially nice and lenient with new children whose approval is important. I personally cannot imagine the kind of pain this must cause children of all ages, but especially adolescents, who are already having a hard enough time just because of their new status as a teenager.

What to do.

What can you do for these teenaged grandchildren? Showing empathy is one of the best services you can provide. The idea of empathy is not knowing what it's like to be the grandchild, but being interested in having him tell you the truth about what it's like and then listening to his account, no matter how hard it is to hear, whom he blames most (rightly or wrongly) for his misery, and what he's afraid of – such as being entirely shut out of the parents' new families, getting beat up every day by bullies, or succumbing to the lure of drugs. Tell him that yes, he's going through a very difficult time, and ask him what options he has for making it better in any way at all. If he cannot think of any, make some gentle suggestions. Such as:

- Running the tension off every day. Or playing a rigorous sport. (Tennis is so great if the child has any talent for it at all.)
- Telling his parents calmly what behaviors he doesn't like. (Let him practice on you.)
- Finding a camp to attend, or get a job at, in the summer. You can help a great deal in this search.
- Planning his career. Finding volunteer work that will help him get jobs and scholarships in his field later on.

And you, Grandmother (or Grandfather) should be:

- Always glad to see him.
- Willing to talk to him for as long as he needs, also to play board games with him and read him books. One great-grandmother I know got her seventeen-year-old through his parents' terrible divorce by having him live with her and reading him books about mythology after dinner every night. Steering him as much as possible away from videogames and TV, especially shows showing happy families. Finding him a good counselor, if he doesn't have one already. What is a good counselor? One who will use the same strategies – listening and helping him find his own options for dealing with the situation – that I just urged you to do.
- Finally, talk to him all the time. Be the one adult who cares consistently what his life is like and finds him important enough to talk to, individually, as much as you have the time to talk and he to listen. Rudeness seldom flourishes in such conditions.

Chapter Twenty-Two

Caring for Plants, Animals and Things

D R. CALMES SAYS this strategy is more important than it sounds. It means, simply, showing children that non-human animals and things in your family are valuable. Dogs, cats, gerbils, ferrets, fish and mice are worth feeding and grooming well and taking for shots. Plants are worth watering and cleaning. Homes are worth polishing and painting and dusting. You know what I mean. Grandparents are good at these things.

By openly, and obviously valuing these non-human accouterments that the child loves, you are also valuing the child.

The child, no matter what her age, can help with this caring and that helping will provide both of you with lots of loving memories and opportunities to teach.

One huge value of this strategy is that it enables the grandparents to become teachers. Haven't you always wanted to be a teacher? Of a class of a few loving pupils who hang on your every word? Now is your chance.

I remember my father teaching my son how to dig postholes and wash and polish a car. My mother taught him how to make wonderful salads and weed flower beds. Both taught him how to read maps during the road trips they took with him.

My friend Sarah teaches her grandchildren homemaking, car care, gardening and antique jewelry polishing, among all the other skills that go into caring for plants, animals and non-living things. Now she's teaching them how to make lovely ceramic pieces that are used as centerpieces, photo frames and other objects of use. She takes them to a pottery center where they always have a great time.

My grandchildren's other grandmother is a horticulturist of great renown. She's showing Gia and Maria the value of beautifying the home with flowers and plants – and caring for them every day.

Just be patient when you show your caring for plants, animals and non-living things and in the teaching of your grandchildren to do these caring tasks. As they learn, they achieve a greater respect for everything and everyone around them.

Chapter Twenty-Three

Show Genuine Love
and Concern

O H, COME ON!" You are saying at this point. "You think that I do not know how to show love and concern for my grandchildren? I'm a grandparent! That's what we do, for gosh sakes!"

I'm not saying you do not have genuine love and concern for your grandchildren. I'm just saying that in the course of daily life, you may not be showing it. Here's a little quiz that will help you find out. Give yourself one point for every "yes" answer.

- When Tiffany is a bit slow about finishing some chore, do you say, "That's it, honey. I'll do it myself"?
- When Jason spills the juice he is trying to pour into everyone's glass, do you throw up your hands in impatience?
- If Brittany squashed your painted egg as she picked it up to show a friend, would you yell at her angrily, telling her she should have known better than to touch it to begin with?
- If Jason, Brittany and Tiffany interrupt you when you're talking on the telephone, do

you tell them to leave you alone, you're busy?

- If you're supposed to pick up Jason at ballet and you are running a few minutes late, do you decide Jason will just have to wait while you do another scheduled errand en route?

A "yes" answer to any of these questions means you need a bit more work on showing love and concern. All these situations demonstrate to the child that he or she is lower than tops on your list of favorites.

The ways people choose to show genuine love and concern are really quite personal. I can't tell you how to perform this feat. I can tell you, however, that if you don't feel genuine love and concern for your grandchildren, don't pretend that you do. They'll know you're faking – and that's worse than just about anything you can do to them.

If you don't feel as much love and concern for your grandchildren, hey, that's fine. Admit it. Perhaps your maternal and/or paternal instincts ran out when your children grew up. Perhaps you want to move on to rock climbing or skydiving or daytrading, or some other long-anticipated phase of your lives. That's fine. Just don't yell at your grandchildren and don't promise them things that you may not fulfill. Send occasional postcards from the mountains or wherever you are, call once a month, and you'll be fine. At least by keeping your grandchildren abreast of your endeavors, they will still feel a part of your life.

Chapter Twenty-Four

Questions from, and Answers for, Grandparents About Dealing with Backtalk from Grandchildren

Q. My 16-year-old twin grandsons say, "Give me a break, Grandma!" every time I ask them to do anything – get their feet off the coffee table, turn down the television, or keep cardboard under their jalopy, which leaks oil on my driveway. Then they look at each other and roll their eyes.

A. You need to deal with the backtalk first. The next time they say "Give me a break," say that kind of speech is not acceptable and as a result you've decided they will be going home. Then call their parents, if necessary, with this news. Enact the consequence by showing them the door. Ignore their protests, which at that age will probably consist of lots more eye rollings and "I don't believe this" and other comments designed to save faces and hurt you. You'll allow them to visit again when they are willing to accept your standards and speak to you with respect.

Q. *My nine-year-old granddaughter backtalks me if I stop her from watching* Powerpuff Girls. *I hate that show but it's about the only issue we disagree on. Should I give in?*

A. You should not let her backtalk you ever. For any reason. The next time she backtalks you about *Powerpuff Girls* or anything else, enact the four steps. As for giving in on that show, I wouldn't. You should be able to set your own standards of behavior and speech and aesthetic values in your home. That show may not meet any of them and it will not hurt your granddaughter to realize that.

Q. *My little three-year-old granddaughter never backtalks but the older two do. I hate playing favorites and saying the little one can visit but the older ones can't. Are you sure this kind of playing favorites is okay?*

A. If not visiting you is the consequence you've chosen for the older two, yes, you can have the little one over but not the older ones. This strategy is not playing favorites, it is enacting a consequence.

Q. *My other grandparent friends think your* Backtalk *book should never be applied to grandchildren. They say grandchildren are meant to be indulged and spoiled and their rudeness just simply ignored. Is this true?*

A. If your grandparent friends think it is all right to allow their grandchildren to behave rudely, fine. I personally think they are just so besotted with these darlings they don't have the nerve to get firm with them in any way. This weakness is not good for them or the grandchildren.

Q. *So your book is not about how to deal with bad behavior from grandchildren, such as not walking the dog or playing frisbee inside. It's about dealing with backtalk?*

A. Yes. There are plenty of books telling adults how to deal with kids' bad behavior. This book tells you how to deal with their speech. As I said elsewhere, if you deal with their rude speech you often stop the bad behavior that goes with it. However, the opposite does not seem to be true.

Q. *My eight-year-old grandson looks and acts so ashamed of himself when I tell him his backtalk is unacceptable that it tears my heart out. Should I enact a consequence anyway if he feels so badly?*

A. Yes. His "shame" may be his way of protesting the consequence, and an attempt to get you to feel bad for following through on it. If you don't enact the consequence, you'll be rewarding his appearing to feel ashamed of himself, and thus causing him to act that way whenever anyone says anything to him the least bit remonstrative. If he does feel deeply ashamed of himself for upsetting you, he might realize he can avoid feeling that way again by deciding not to backtalk you again. Try saying something like this: "You seemed to feel badly about yourself when I told you the backtalk wasn't acceptable. I bet you don't like feeling that way, and you know, you don't ever need to feel that way again – if you don't backtalk again!"

Q. I believe that children outgrow backtalk if you ignore it. My three children did just that and today, as successful thirty-somethings, they're very respectful adults.

A. Backtalk was different when your children were young. Back then, society in general tended to be more respectful. Influences were more benign. Today's backtalk is more harsh because it's influenced by violent and aggressive music, video games, movies and TV. These are tougher times for kids. Their cultural environment demands that adults apply much more emphasis and structure in helping them deal with this problem.

I found an example of the changes in children's speech in a new commercial for a chocolate drink. For at least 40 years, this product had been advertised by commercials in which happy children drank this product and then pleaded politely in unison, "More (of this product), please!" In the new commercial, the children don't ask for the product, they demand it. A young boy cries out in a harsh, confrontational tone, "(This product) rules!" All semblance of politeness is gone. Now, the old commercial seems hopelessly out-of-date, obsolete.

It's up to adults who deal with these children on a regular basis to teach them that much of this modern speech is unpleasant and hurtful and will not be tolerated.

Q. *What can happen to a child who's allowed to backtalk all she wants?*

A. Here are a few of the possibilities.

- She may fail to develop the ability to care what other people think, feel and want.

- Her future relationships may be adversely affected.
- She could become bored with people who love and need her.
- She might increase her tendency to make conversations confrontational.

Not that such types are always unbearable. Hyacinth on the British sitcom *Keeping Up Appearances,* is hilarious if you don't have to live with, or next door to, her. Roseanne was outrageous in her insistence on being her belligerent self, and my cousin's wife Mae is saintly as a committed environmentalist who demands everyone share her views and her rigid conservation practices. Let's face it, in order to make the most of your relationship with your granddaughter, you must both respect each other. Her treating you with disrespect is one of the most painful possibilities.

Q. *I've just finished reading your manuscript and I'm confused about one thing. How can I be a nice grandmother all the time, and still deal with grandchildren's unwanted backtalk?*

A. Dealing with backtalk using the four steps does not mean getting mad. It means maintaining a neutral attitude as you announce and enact the consequence. The child may be upset at this neutral reaction because he wants you to react. A reacting adult is a controlled adult! But deep down, he'll find comfort in your inner strength and power to resist his attempts to manipulate your mood.

Q. *I really don't understand why you should not let a grandchild know how hurt you are when he backtalks. If you feel hurt, shouldn't you show it?*

A. If you have a very close, loving relationship with your grandchild, yes; you can show how hurt you are at his rudeness–the first time. The guilt he feels then might be enough to stop any more backtalk ever again.

A woman I met on a train told me her five-year-old grandson was so devastated by the obvious pain he caused her the first time he was rude to her that he cried for hours. "He couldn't even talk, he was so upset," she recalled. "Finally, before bed that night, he looked up at me with these big, teary eyes and said, 'Oh, Mimi'–that's what he called me–'you have my heart.' Well, of course, I just took him up in a big bear hug and laughed and cried and told him I forgave him completely. He has not ever been rude to me since and this was almost a year ago." I was teary-eyed myself at this point, and hearing imaginary violins playing in the background.

An issue with showing your hurt feelings is that, although you can be fairly sure your grandchild may feel guilty about causing you pain, you know that his guilt, much like your pain, will subside. Unless he truly learns consequences of backtalking, and learns to stop it, he's still likely to try backtalk again in the future. Only the next time, he may not be so sensitive to your pain.

The idea with your grandchildren is to be loving and caring but strong, a force to be respected, instead of an easy mark. The four steps to dealing with backtalk help you project this kind of strength, without having to become angry or melodramatic yourself.

Chapter Twenty-Five

Special
Situations

I REALIZE THAT NOT all grandparents have perfect lives. Here are ways of dealing with grandchildren and their backtalk for those in some of the most common unwanted conditions.

Grandparents who have to be parents:
Recently, I saw a nice-looking couple with white hair wheeling three small children up to a grocery store in a grocery cart they must have kept at their house, which must have been nearby. On more careful observation, I saw that, nicely groomed as they were, this couple looked stooped and tired, and their clothes were just a bit worn. The children seemed happy enough but could have used some haircombing. There was a sense of fatigue and struggle against despair in the scene, that was oddly disturbing. Later, I realized the couple was probably raising those children, not just acting as grandparents. That must have been why there was no car, and no time for careful brushing of hair in this family. It was also why there was no

happy Ensure-ad type energy to be seen on the grandparents' faces. At a time in their lives when they had earned the right to enjoy life and their grandkids, they were repeating the entire parenting role over again, from scratch. It is not fair. But, the teachers I interviewed told me, it is happening more and more. Many more of their students are now being raised by grandparents than ever before.

How should live-in grandchildren's backtalk be handled? The same way any child's backtalk is handled. The first *Backtalk* book is needed by these grandparents more than this book!

Grandparents who do not want to be grandparents

Once I had a friend whose mother told her daughter never to call her "Grandmother" but to address her always by her first name, instead. *No* one was allowed to call this woman a grandmother, in fact. She was married to a famous writer, and known for her domestic skills, and just not intending to take on the grandmotherly role. She was not interested in hearing about her granddaughter at all, or seeing her or playing with her.

Here's the point of telling you this story: I'm not here to say this grandmother is bad. She cannot help the way she feels. I'm here to tell you that if you fit this description (which is hard to imagine, since you have read this far in this book) or can identify with the way this woman feels, you need to be warned. You are missing one of life's greatest joys. No matter how you feel, get to know your grandchildren as people as soon as you can. You need them in order to stay young in a vibrant, connected sort of way.

Grandparents who suddenly find themselves step-grandparents:

You were happily enjoying your own grandchildren when your son or daughter marries someone with one or more children from previous marriages. If you are like other grandparents I've known in this situation, you will be inundated with requests for baby-sitting, and will be urged strongly to love these new grandchildren as your own. Barbecues, camping trips and other activities involving you and the new brood will be arranged, to promote the instant happy family feeling your adult child and his/her spouse are so eager to create.

My advice is, go slowly. Get to know the new kids one at a time, not in groups. Show your own grandchildren they are just as important to you as ever. Read this book again and again, because stepchildren and grandchildren, bless their little hearts, will use backtalk as a way of showing everyone how tough they are. Use consequences as usual (remember, backtalk is never justified, no matter how hurt the child), but help the child find other ways of communicating feelings of loss, resentment, jealously, and rage that divorce and remarriage almost always mean for kids.

When backtalk occurs on a car trip:

Grandparents love taking grandchildren on auto trips. They especially love taking them on "exploration" auto trips, where the goal is the exploration of a city or place, such as the Grand Canyon or San Francisco or Indian ruins. But alas, grandchildren today can be rude on these trips, thus rendering them more work than fun.

Examples of backtalk on car trips:
- "Of course, I can see those cows, Grandma! Do you think I've never seen a cow before?"
- "God you drive slow, Grandpa! At least go the speed limit or we'll never get where we're going."
- "What? You're stopping at a vegetable stand? Are you high? There's a McDonald's a few more miles up the road, I just saw the sign."

- "This is the eighth time you made me take off these headphones, Grandmother! Can't you see I'm really into this music?"

These backtalk responses are disagreeable, unpleasant, and can hurt. You've been planning this trip for a long time, you've already spent a great deal of money on it, and now, your excitement is turning to dread.

Act now, when the backtalk first begins, and the rest of your trip may be terrific. Here are some consequence ideas that have been known to work:

Consequences that can be used in the car:
- Pull over, stop, and announce that the that kind of speech is unacceptable on the trip. "That kind of speech is unacceptable As a result, we will not be eating at McDonald's." To the ensuing protest, you say only, "Maybe we can try again tomorrow."
- Announce that this speech is not acceptable and as a result, you will not buy the child any souvenirs at the next gift shop stop.
- Announce that this speech is not acceptable and as a result, the amount of spending money the child will get will be

docked $10.00. (Or however much you think will be most effective.)

Ways of preventing backtalk on car trips:

I strongly urge you to schedule a trip-planning session with the grandchildren before the traveling. At this planning session, present the itinerary, and negotiate with them the sights you expect to take them to (and tell why they'll be interesting), the amount of souvenirs they will be bought by you en route, and the amount of spending money they'll get, at what points on the trip Let them choose the kinds of restaurants where you'll be eating en route, and the kinds of lodging they'll most enjoy. (They'll have a great time looking up hotels and motels and comparing sizes of pools, heights of water slides, number of channels on in-room TV's and other amenities meant to appeal to kids.) If they're able to read well enough, they should receive travel books about your destination city so they can choose sites of interest themselves. Discuss limiting the amount of time they can use headphones and walkmen. You don't want to end up shouting, "Take off those head phones! I'm trying to tell you something!" every time you want to converse with your grandchildren on this trip.

Do discuss ground rules you care about, i.e., that their communication and behavior on this trip needs to be pleasant and agreeable, or consequences will occur. But don't dwell on this issue during the planning session. The tone in which you conduct these planning sessions should be as upbeat and excited as the trip itself.

Never forget: traveling by automobile is a wonderful idea for grandparents and grandchildren. The kids learn patience, pleasure in visual sights (such as the way haystacks look against a cloudy gray sky) and homespun attractions (such as a church bazaar in another town) and local history (the Douglas MacArthur museum in Norfolk, Virginia is incredible, as is the Liberace museum in Las Vegas.) These out-of-the ordinary experiences will create memories the grandchildren will cherish and tell *their* grandchildren about for the rest of their lives.

Chapter Twenty-Six

Workbook

YOU DON'T HAVE to use a workbook But it helps.

Just do not feel guilty if you start one and stop using it regularly. You can use the following workbook techniques whenever you want.

What to buy:

Get yourself a thick notebook and a small notebook that can fit in your purse or pocket. Use the smaller one for jotting down backtalk when it happens (record date and time and place) and consequences chosen and words you used when enacting them.

What to do:

In the big notebook, just simply keep a diary of your time with your grandchildren. Put the date at the top of the page, then write about the events of the day, including the backtalk. Tell the who, what, when, where, why and how of the incident and how you implemented, or failed to implement the four steps. End the day's entry with a paragraph or two on your feelings about the whole episode.

Instead of telling you how to fill out your notebook categories of Who, What, When, Where, Why and How, I am going to give you this hypothetical example of a grandmother's Workbook entry:

June 15

We all went to the water park today, Lynn, Louis, Lori and I.

- *Who (backtalked):*
  Louis did it when I asked him to sit down on the water slide in the proper way.
- *Where the backtalk took place:*
  At the water slide. I was watching the children slide down when I saw Louis was sitting on the slide backward, facing the opposite direction. The rules posted nearby specifically said the slide users must sit facing the slide.
- *What (the backtalk consisted of and what consequence was chosen):*
  He screamed when I yelled up at him to turn around, "I can sit anyway I want!" Then he went down the slide backward. That was backtalk. The consequence for him I chose was not going with us that night to the movies. When he came out of the slide, I said, "Louis, that kind of speech is not acceptable. As a result, you'll be staying home with Grandfather this

evening when the rest of us go to the movies." The protest he gave was pretty bad, full of yelling, until a lifeguard told him he'd have to control himself or leave. He was quieter after that and I guess had a good time until we left around four.

- *When (Step Two, Enacting the Consequence) took place:*
The consequence was enacted that night. We all got ready to go to the movies, including Louis, and it was a little hard to tell him that he would not be joining us. But I did it, in a very calm way that I was proud of. I called from the movie theater an hour later to see how Louis was doing and Martin said they were playing Scrabble and eating cheese popcorn.

- *Why (the consequence was chosen and that backtalk happened):*
I don't know why Louis spoke to me so rudely. He backtalks other people a lot, not just me and I'm glad I've found a way of dealing with it. I'm afraid he has some sort of emotional control problem. I'll speak to his parents about it. That particular consequence was chosen because all the children had been looking forward to the movies. They love going to the movies and I always let them have all the popcorn and soda they want. Not

being able to go to the movies was a consequence I know Louis did not want. Although I wonder if maybe he did not need time alone with his grandfather. Or me or any adult.

- *How (the consequence worked):*
  I think it worked at least for today, because Louis has not backtalked me or his grandfather since I announced the consequence.

- *What I would do differently next time:*
  I think I would try to remain more calm when announcing the consequence. I got mad when Louis yelled at me, and I'm not good when I get mad, I'm a kind of banshee, almost out of control. OR: I would choose a different consequence next time, a more immediate one such as taking everyone home right then. Louis' backtalk was very hurtful and needed an immediate response.

Note: The following category is good to add if you tend to have anxiety about other backtalk situations cropping up.

- *What I worry about:*
  What if the other kids had started backtalking, too, after I announced the consequence? I know – I could have just

called off the movie trip altogether. What if Louis had pouted all evening and given his grandfather a bad time? I could have told Martin to ignore him. (You get the idea.)

Or just write.

Or just write a narrative account of the backtalk event, making sure you cover as many facets of it as possible.

Keep at it.

When you start out with a particular workbook style, use it at least for three entries before switching to another style. Sometimes, you need to refine a style in order to make it work for you, and you can only do that with practice.

Use the smaller notebook all the time.

You absolutely should try to jot down the backtalk facts when they happen, just as you jot down an item you need on your shopping list, or a new appointment in your appointment calendar, at that moment. This recording of the backtalk as soon after it happens as possible will also help you maintain your neutral attitude toward it.

Think about this added benefit:

Here's a final selling point for the workbook: if it's legible enough, and does not contain too many profanities, it can be a wonderful heirloom for your grandchildren to inherit, and to use in raising their children.

But...

But if you want to use the workbook just for yourself, for no one else's eyes but your own, that is fine, too!

Annotated List of Resources

I am not going to list a lot of books here. The few that I do want to bring to your attention do not necessarily fit the category of self-help book, but provide perspectives on parenting that I want to share.

How to Talk So Kids Can Learn at Home and at School, by Adele Faber and Elaine Mazlish (1996, Simon and Schuster/ Fireside). This book is extremely helpful in dealing with kids who, for various reasons, live in such a state of anxiety that they are always saying the wrong thing.

Can't Buy Me Love, by Sally Coleman and Nancy Hull-Mast. (1992, Compcare Publishers). If you are spending too much money on your grandchildren and cannot stop, you might find this book very helpful.

Driven to Distraction: Recognizing and Coping with Attention Deficit Disorder from Childhood through Adulthood, by Edward M. Hallowell and John J. Ratey (1994, Simon and Schuster/Touchstone). If you suspect you or your children or your grandchildren might have this disorder to some degree, you will find this book extremely reassuring and helpful. Both authors are medical doctors who understand prescription medications for ADD as well as management of this condition.

A Cup of Christmas Tea, by Tom Hegg, Illustrated by Warren Hansen (1992, Wald House). This beautifully illustrated book is written in fun-to-read rhyme. In a lovely, nonjudgmental way, it teaches appreciation of older relatives who may have been forgotten in the rush of every day life.

Backtalk: Four Steps to Ending Rude Behavior in Kids, by Audrey Ricker and Carolyn Crowder (1998, Simon and Schuster/ Firestone). Please read the reviews of this book found on the Amazon.com website.

APPENDIX

Consequence Ideas
for Different Age Groups

Ways of Announcing
the Consequences

Lessons Your Grandchildren
Will Learn from Your
Consequences

The Calmes' Plan Revisited

How to Start a Grandparent
Support Group

Dear Grandma,

     I hope you feel better soon. I wish that they never would have had to do the test in your leg. Maybe when it heels we can spend a fun day together. Maybe breakfast at your house, than lunch at Austin's, a movie, and chicken at your house. Does that sound fun to you? Do you think we can do that?

Love,
Michelle

Here's another letter to Audrey Marcus written by her granddaughter, Michelle, almost a year after she wrote the letter published on page 2.

Appendix

Here are ideas for consequences for different age groups.

Toddlers: (about two to four)

I know, I said grandparents are incapable of interpreting toddlers' speech as backtalk. I've since been informed by readers of this book that some grandchildren are born backtalkers and need the four steps from a very early age. If this is true of your grandchild, try announcing these consequences in these ways:

- "That kind of talk is not polite (or good or nice or whatever word you prefer that you know the child will understand right away). I'm going to stop coloring with you (or playing a game or driving to a favorite pizza place or watching a video or doing whatever it is you are doing with the child that the child usually enjoys) right now."
- "That kind of talk is not acceptable (I believe that the younger a child is when he is spoken to with a complex vocabulary,

the better his vocabulary will be.) I'm taking Cousin Kenny home right now." Or, "We're leaving playgroup (or Aunt Jenny's birthday party or wherever you are that the child had wanted to be) right now."

Here's a classic case history involving a toddler and his grandmother:

My friend Beth is the main babysitter for her two-year-old grandson, Edgar, while her daughter works evenings. Every afternoon, Beth picks Edgar up from his daycare center and sees to it he had his dinner. Often, she takes him out to eat at either his favorite place, the Pizza Arcade, or at her favorite place, the Oriental Rice Bowl.

One evening as they were driving to the Rice Bowl, little Edgar told Beth that he refused to go to the Rice Bowl, that he demanded they go to the Pizza Arcade instead. Upon being reminded by Beth that they had eaten at the Pizza place three times that week and it was now her turn to eat where she wanted, Edgar called his grandmother a "stupid dummy" and began repeating these words in a screaming tone. Though usually enchanted by Edgar's efforts to assert himself, Beth did not find this "stupid dummy" label amusing and decided it was backtalk. "You may not say such things to me," she informed him. "We are going right home now." And she drove back to her house, ignoring Edgar's screams and kicking and throwing of everything he could find within reach of his carseat. When she pulled up to her home, she heard Edgar say in a very subdued voice, "Go to Rice Bowl, Grandma." Anything was better to Edgar than eating at home.

But it was too late. "Maybe tomorrow, Edgar," Beth said, in a neutral tone. "Maybe we can try the Rice Bowl tomorrow."

They did eat at the Rice Bowl the following night. Edgar was very agreeable about this choice of restaurants from the time they entered the place til, full of sweet and sour tofu and rice, he fell asleep on the way home.

Here are some more backtalk choices and examples of announcement. The choices indicated for age groups are just suggestions; you can certainly use a consequence meant for an older child with a younger one–and vice versa.

Age four to eight:
- "That kind of talk is not acceptable. As a result, I'm not turning on the television until tomorrow morning."
- "That kind of talk is not acceptable. As a result, we're taking you home this evening

(or as soon as Mommy comes home from work or wherever she is) instead of tomorrow."

- "That kind of talk is not acceptable. As a result, we're not going to McDonald's for lunch."
- "That kind of talk is not acceptable. As a result, I'm going to stop playing this game with you immediately."

Age eight to ten:

- "That kind of talk is not acceptable. As a result, I'm not buying you the CD I promised to buy you this afternoon.."
- "That kind of talk is not acceptable. As a result, I'm not going to take you to the park or playground today."
- "That kind of talk is not acceptable. As a result, we're not going to Cousin Amy's birthday party today."
- "That kind of talk is unacceptable. As a result, we're leaving Cousin Amy's party immediately."

Age ten to 15:

Notice the use of the word "motivated" starts with this age group. But you can certainly use it with children of younger ages if you feel comfortable doing so.

- "That kind of talk is unacceptable. As a result, we're not going to the pool today."
- "That kind of talk is unacceptable. As a result, I'm not motivated to buy you the new outfit (or CD or video game or whatever) I promised you today."
- "That kind of talk is unacceptable. As a result, I'm not motivated to let you use the cell phone today."

Age 15 to 20:
- "That kind of talk is unacceptable. As a result, we're not motivated to let you use the car today."
- "That kind of talk is unacceptable. As a result, I'm not motivated to help pay (any or part of) your summer camp. (Or private school or class trip.)" This consequence may seem harsh, but at this age, it's very important to send a strong message quickly.

Age 20 on:
- "That kind of talk is unacceptable. As a result, I'm not motivated to baby-sit any of your children this weekend."
- "That kind of talk is unacceptable. As a result, I'm not motivated to water your plants while you're away."
- "That kind of talk is unacceptable. As a result, I'm not motivated to come over for

dinner (or have you over for dinner) this week."

Here's what you will be teaching by choosing and implementing these consequences with the kind of language suggested here:
- Backtalk hurts.
- It is not all right to hurt others when the mood strikes.
- Respect for others is important.
- You are motivated to do wonderful things for your grandchildren when you are treated respectfully. But you are not motivated to expend your time, money and energy on them when you are spoken to disrespectfully.
- You are not waiting around hoping they'll decide to be nice to you.
- You have other things in your life you can turn to besides the grandchildren.
- People, including loving people, have limits on the kinds of behavior they will tolerate.

Even you, the person who loves them most unconditionally, have your limits. That must mean, your grandchildren will then figure out, bosses and teachers have limits, too. *Remember:* The only response you can ever make to the protest of these consequences is,

"Maybe we can try again tomorrow," and shrug as though you don't know. Don't say one word more. The child knows you mean that if his speech is polite from then on, he may get the consequence rescinded tomorrow.

**How to avoid harshness
when announcing your consequence:**
You can precede your announcement with a "Sweetpea," or "Honey," or some other endearing term Just don't let allow this sweetness to interfere with your non-negotiating position.

How to keep calm when the backtalk hits:
- Take a deep breath, hold eight seconds, exhale to the count of eight. *Remember:* Reactions are useless without enactment of a consequence. (Unless, of course, your grand-child is a saint who cannot bear to see you feel bad.)
- If you don't have a consequence to use this time, ignore the backtalk. Excuse yourself and start making lists of consequences to use next time the backtalk happens.

**The Calmes' Plan
for a Rudeness-Free Home:**
- Model the kind of behavior you expect from your grandchildren at all times.

- Be consistent in your rudeness free attitudes and consideration of others.
- Reinforce behavior in others that you enjoy.
- Show care for animals, plants and property. (That means showing appreciation for the animals, plants and property you already have, not buying new ones when the old ones get difficult, wilt or suffer neglect.)
- Show empathy for grandchildren who are coping with difficulties (this group can include just about all children in this day and age.)
- Show genuine care and concern for all living things. (If you can't own any living things, volunteer at nursing homes, at pet shelters and children's hospitals, taking your grandchildren with you.)

Starting a support group for grandparents with backtalking grandchildren:
Such groups can be enormously helpful (you'll find you are not the only grandparent with backtalking children) and lots of fun.

1. Put a notice on a recreation room bulletin board, in the association newsletter or in the local paper that says, "Grandparents! Let's get together and talk about

grandchildren's behavior!" Then give the time, date, and place you decide on. Or just send invitations to friends who are grandparents.

2. When the meeting convenes, state that the purpose is to discuss ways of dealing with grandchildren's backtalk and other rude behavior. Don't be upset if only one other person is present, two can form a very productive support group!

3. Ask for examples of backtalking and/or rude kinds of behavior from grandchildren. Let everyone who wants to contribute.

4. Now ask what everyone did in response to the rude behavior, followed by two questions. Did these responses work to stop the behavior? How did the grandparent feel afterward?

5. Now discuss the four steps and consequence ideas from this book.

6. Entertain other suggestions for dealing with backtalk.

7. Be a gracious but in-control group leader. Caution! I have learned that you will encounter grandparents who are against any less-than- indulgent treatment of grandchildren for any reason. These types will say, often in a self-righteous, superior tone, "Oh, I could *never* do *that!*" when a consequence is discussed.

Here's what you can do to handle these types: Point out that these grandparents have a different agenda from the rest of you: They seem to want to get the grandkids' approval more than they want to teach them respect for others. Then ask the other group members if they agree with what you just said. A lively discussion will probably ensue.

8. If the meeting goes well, set a regular meeting time and date, and ask members how they feel about using this book as a text. If they are willing, ask them to buy this book (bookstores may provide group discounts) and have certain chapters read by the next meeting. Or, if members prefer and you are willing, collect the money for the books and buy them yourself for the next meeting.

For more immediate help with any of these topics:

Contact Audrey Ricker and/or Robert E. Calmes at *ricker@u.arizona.edu* or contact them through Amagansett Publishers.

Index

A

activities
  to avoid, 52-53
  recommended, 51, 79-80, 87-88, 114, 115, 118
adult backtalk, 14
adventure walks, 80
age backtalk begins, 11
animals, caring for, 117-118
Anne of Green Gables, 101
announcements vs. threats, 40
answers, to questions, 123-130
appropriate response to backtalk, 13
atmosphere, 91-92
attitude
  neutral, 128-129
  positive, 96-97

B

Backtalk: Four Steps to Ending Rude Behavior in Your Kids, 3, 7, 8, 14, 17, 29, 36, 38, 45, 79, 132, 146
backtalk vs. disagreement, 26-27
backtalk vs. honest expression, 27-28
behavior, modeling, 14, 73-75, 99-103
blame, 105, 106
budget, 77-81, 96

C

Calmes, Robert E., 91, 95, 105, 117, 158
Can't Buy Me Love, 145
caring for animals and plants, 117-118
car trips, 134-137
causes of backtalk, 4
choosing a consequence, 16-17, 29-38
Coleman, Sally, 145
communication, 115
compromise, 63-64
concern, demonstrating, 119-121
consequences
  to avoid, 33-34
  big, 34-35
  for car trips, 135-136
  choosing, 16-17, 29-38
  enacting, 17-18, 39-42
  requirements of, 32-33
  for various ages, 149-158

consistency, 93-97
criticism, 62-63
Crowder, Carolyn, 146
Cup of Christmas Tea, A, 146

D
deciding on a consequence, 16-17, 29-38
demonstrating love and concern, 119-121
diabetes, 71
disagreement vs. backtalk, 29-27
disengaging from protest, 18-19, 43-47
divorce, 113
Driven to Distraction, 145-146

E
empathy, 111-115
enacting a consequence, 17-18, 39-42
environment, 91-92
epistolary-type novel, 80
exercise, see physical activity

F
Faber, Adele, 145
failure vs. success, 105
favorites, playing, 83-86, 124

finances, 77-81, 96
forms of backtalk, 11-12, 25-26
Four Step Program, 15-20
see also choosing a consequence; disengaging from protest; enacting a consequence; recognizing backtalk

G
generosity, 96
getting a life, 53, 55-58
gifts, 80-81
grandparents in parenting role, 131-132

H
Hallowell, Edward M., 145
Hegg, Tom, 146
Holistic Parenting, 71
honest expression vs. backtalk, 27-28
How to Talk So Kids Can Learn at Home and at School, 145
Hull-Mast, Nancy, 145
hypoglycemia, 71

I
ignoring protest, 18-19, 43-47
inappropriate response to backtalk, 13-14

interests, obtaining your own, 53, 55-58

L
language of reinforcement, 108
life, getting one, 53, 55-58
love, demonstrating, 119-121
low-cost ideas, 79-80

M
Mazlish, Elaine, 145
media, 99-103
Miracle Worker, The, 19
modeling behavior
   see behavior, modeling
money, 77-81, 96
mood, 95
music videos, 100-101

N
negative reinforcement, 108-109
notebook, 139-144
nurturing plants and animals, 117-118
nutrition, 69-71

P
physical activity, 87-88, 101-102, 114
plants, caring for, 117-118

playing favorites, 83-86, 124
positive attitude, 96-97
positive reinforcement, 105-109
praise vs. blame, 105
projects, 79-80.
   see also activities
protest, disengaging from, 18-19, 43-47
punishment, 105, 107

Q
questions and answers, 123-130

R
Ratey, John J., 145
reaction to backtalk, 13-14
reading, to grandchildren, 101
reasons for backtalk, 4
recognizing backtalk, 11-12, 21-28
recommended activities
   see activities
reinforcement, 105-109
reluctant grandparents, 132-133
research, conducting your own, 65-67
resources, 145-146
response to backtalk, 13-14

rewards, 105, 106-107
Ricker, Audrey, 146
 contact information, 158
role models, 99-103
role of grandparent, 75,
   93, 115
routine, 96
rules
   for car trips, 137
   for grandparent/child
   relationship, 3, 75 (see
   also role of
   grandparent)
   setting your own, 65-
   66

S
showing love and
   concern, 119-121
situations, special, 131-
   137
Sneyd, Lynn Wiese, 71
social life
   of grandchildren, 96
   of grandparent, 53,
   55-58
special situations,
   131-137
sports. see physical
   activity
standards
   consistency of, 95
   setting your own,
   61-64
stepfamilies, 113

stepgrandparents,
   133-134
success vs. failure, 105
sugar pushing, 52, 69-71

T
teachers, 65-67
teenagers, 111-115
threats vs. announcements,
   40
tolerance, 73-75
   see also compromise
types of backtalk, 11-12,
   25-26

V
videogames, 99-100
volunteering, 114

W
Winfrey, Oprah, 94
workbook, 139-144
wrong response to
   backtalk, 13-14